NAKED AND DIMED

MY LIFELONG QUEST FOR AWESOME TONE

RAM W. TULI

IN MEMORY OF "HELLHOUND" DAVID HULL
(1958 - 2015)

Table of Contents

ACKNOWLEDGMENTS

I would like to thank Tommie James, Michael Clark, John Peden, Paul Linden, Pat Geraghty, Dave Hunter, Nic Grabien, Greg Perrine, Harvey Moltz, Gil Southworth Jr., Tom Guerra, Mike Simpson, Dave Stephens, Jeff Smith, Timm Kummer, Kim Shaheen, Willie Smith, Rich Taylor, Binky Philips, Kevin Kelly, Jeff Travis, Antoine Gedroyc, James Borkowitz, Terry Selfe, Mick Flynn, Lowell Hunt, Willard Lewis Snow, Vic DePra, Bill Cleeland, Hector Barrera, Tony Whelan, John Markovich, Randy Volin, Philip Benton, Nacho Banos, Robb Lowe, Eliot Michael, Burke Hunn, Deke Dickerson, Doug Van Quekelberg, Don Mare, Nic Koff, Larry Briggs, Bryan Wells, Mark Daven, Scott Braker-Abene, Dan Astor, Ben Prevo, Mike Benny Powell, Donny Craven, Joe Riggio, Don Lee, Albi Duarte, Robert Randolph, Kim Holloway, Clayton W. Munsey, Scott Kaye, John Holcomb, Nathan Ballein, Joe Pampel, Jeff Johnson, Dennis Fano, Robert Mondell, Bill Brott, Francesco Balossino, Drew Berlin, Mike Reeder, Michael Slubowski, Harold Henkel, John Stokes, Nicky V. Hines, Gregory Teves, and the countless others who talk guitars and amps with me all day long.

A special shout out to my Moojmates, Richard Chavez, Rick Obenshain, and Shane Matsumoto for another incredible mind-melting studio adventure.

I'd like to also thank my good friend, Joel Klein. He was instrumental in getting this project completed.

FOREWORD

I joined my first band in November of 1960. My amp then was a rent-to-own 1960 Fender 5F6-A tweed Bassman. I paid it off in 2 years and then got a new 1961 Fender 6G12-A brown/wheat Concert amp. Both had 4x10 speakers, sounded great, but were very different. I wondered why. Thus, began a life-long quest for that "perfect tone," you know ... searching for that sound that feels "just right" for the song you're playing.

Over the years I have owned, recorded, and gigged with over a hundred amps, mostly Fenders, that included everything from small Deluxes and Harvards to huge Showmans and Twin Reverbs. Also included was a Gibson, several Ampegs, Kustom heads and cabinets, and boutiques from Benson, Clark, and Fullertone.

In the 1990s I began to learn more about amps by reading books and articles, and got some great help from Michael Clark who had been the sound-man in my band for much of the 1980s. After he repaired the '60 Bassman and '61 Concert, he convinced me to let him replace the filter, bias, and by-pass caps, and then install matched NOS power and pre-amp tubes in both. Those old amps came back to life in a way I never thought I'd hear again. It was then that I began experimenting with using different tubes & speakers. I found magic combinations for each and discovered that "perfect tone"... as defined by my ears.

I met Bill Tuli when he purchased one of my vintage Fender amps and was intrigued when he told me about his plan to record a whole album using different guitars and amps, and isolate the tracks so each combination could be easily heard and compared. With his electrical engineering background, he understood the technical details of his amps but wanted to dig deeper into finding out what really made them so special. His musical virtuosity and years of playing made him uniquely qualified to undertake this project.

Naked and Dimed features rare vintage instruments and amps with photos and detailed descriptions including how they were recorded and an evaluation of the sound of each. Also included is the result of the author's extensive research on vintage instrument and amp values and how they have changed over the years. It informs and entertains unlike any other that has been penned and published to date.

Tommie James
Engineer, musician, collector & restorer of fine vintage amps,
Camden, SC USA

INTRODUCTION

No, *Naked and Dimed* isn't the title of some naughty movie you saw listed on the Mitchell Brothers sign when you were a kid. It's the name of the latest Psychedelic Mooj album. By "naked" we mean nothing came between guitar and amp (well, besides a cord). We didn't use one stomp box on anything. What you hear is what we got straight out of each amp.

In the old days "dimed" meant loud—turned up to *10* loud. The hep-cats who came before us used a different expression because their amps went to 12. They called it "clockwising the chickenhead to the max." Since only four of the amps we used had chickenheads, we'll just stick with "dimed."

In reality, only a few of the amps were actually recorded at full volume. I love playing my amps totally cranked. However, when we got in the studio and tweaked things to sound "best," many volume knobs ended up being closer to the point of breakup (6 to 8) than 10 or 12. I guess we should have called the album *Naked and Nearly Clockwise Chickenheaded and Dimed,* but then you'd have really been confused.

It's our hope that *Naked and Dimed* will go into the history books as the most "vintage" album ever recorded. With the exception of two guitars, everything used on the project was at least 35 years old. In fact, most of it was well over 50. Everything was as close to original as possible.

We've used vintage guitars on previous Psychedelic Mooj albums, but never more than one or two amps. On *Naked and Dimed*, we used 14 amps. You read that right—14. This album was all about exploring the tone and textures of vintage Fender amplifiers. We used one non-Fender amp, an Ampeg B-18-N (mounted atop a B-15 cabinet). That was for bass only. Surely, you'll forgive us for that.

I've been a tone purist since the beginning. Even when I only knew the riff to "Smoke on the Water" and the intro to "Stairway to Heaven," I realized there was a reason why Jimi Hendrix, Eric Clapton, Duane Allman, Jimmy Page, Michael Bloomfield, Jeff Beck, Robin Trower, Jimmie and Stevie Ray Vaughn, Roy Buchanan, Billy Gibbons, *etal.* sounded so good. Yes, they were exceptional players, but they also had something the elders called tone. Until recently, I thought all that tone came from their iconic guitars. Thus, for almost 40 years I've pretty much only played Stratocasters, Telecasters, and Les Pauls. Just try and hand me whatever the kids use today and I'll politely decline. It's nothing personal. It's just that my generation was indoctrinated to play only Fenders and Gibsons. *But,* here's the odd thing: as uncompromising as I was about guitars, I was never that fussy about my amp. I figured if it was a tube amp, that's all that mattered. This, of course, was a *huge* misconception. I now know that most of my sonic character is colored and shaped by whatever amplifier I'm plugged into. I didn't realize this before because my first true gigging rig was a 1967 black-face Fender Super Reverb. To me, that amp was just a massive sound support system for a little yellow overdrive pedal. Any guitar I played through it sounded incredible. I figured *all* tube amps sounded like that.

The old Super Reverb was finally put to pasture in 2006 when I became the lead vocalist for The Psychedelic Mooj. The amp still sounded great, but I was getting zapped every time I grabbed the microphone. I just assumed that was the peril of gigging with an old amplifier. (The other being getting a hernia.) It was time to modernize. Like I said, I wasn't that fussy. I shopped around. I tried everything, including hybrids and modelling amps. I stayed true to my roots and settled for a Fender '65 Twin Reverb Re-issue. That 64-pound monolith was agonizingly lugged on and off barroom stages for the next three years and used exclusively on the first two Psychedelic Mooj albums. Like the Super Reverb before it, it was clean, loud, and easily flavored with an overdrive pedal.

The massive Twin Reverb Re-issue was sidelined for a more "back friendly" '65 Deluxe Reverb Re-issue in 2010. I didn't know it then, but that 22-watt wonder launched me on an auditory journey of discovery. Before I knew it, I was exploring the marvels of a low-powered amp. My so-called *Analog Soup* sound (our third album) was built around it.

Then came that figurative lightning bolt to the head. I read Tom Wheeler's *The Soul of Tone: Celebrating 60 Years of Fender Amps.* I always knew my 1967 Super Reverb was a great amp, but I never considered how other Fender amplifiers from that same era might sound. For 30+ years I'd been worrying about such trivialities as: "What sounds better, maple or rosewood necks?" What I really should have been contemplating was how does my guitar flux-generated signal become enlarged and converted into mechanical energy so that my ears can hear it. Was it even worthwhile finding out? Being a purist, I knew how important it was to keep vintage guitars completely original. How was that even possible with a 50- or 60-year-old high voltage suitcase that had been road abused for the past half century?

Then I took the plunge. I saw a 1964 Deluxe Reverb for sale on eBay. It had just been refurbished by Michael Clark and retained most of its original components (the factory-installed 2-prong plug had been swapped for the safer grounded version, Sprague Atoms were now hidden under the original Astron paper sleeves, and the Oxford 12K5-6 had been re-coned). I bid aggressively on the amp and won. I was elated until I saw the dollar damage done. Oh well, that's the danger of placing maximum bids when one has had a beer or two. *But* I was on my way! I was about to find out if my Deluxe Reverb Re-issue sounded anything like the real thing.

The UPS man came and went. I carried my new arrival into the Mooj Cave and carefully extracted the Deluxe Reverb from its oversized, popcorn-filled cardboard box. I removed the bubble-wrapped cocoon and excavated the wadded up newspapers. I was a bit confused. There were no tubes. Ah, they were at the bottom of the amp in colorful NOS boxes. Because I'd been tube-schooled in the U.S. Navy, I put on gloves to insert them. (In the navy, we weren't allowed to touch vacuum tubes with our bare hands, lest we shorten their lives with fingerprint oil). I powered up the Deluxe Reverb. No smoke or burning smell—that was good. I plugged in one of my Stratocasters and nearly lost my mind. My Deluxe Reverb Re-issue was a great amp—*but it never sounded like this!* From that day forward, much to my wife's displeasure, I became an ardent gatherer of Leo Fender's incredible finger-jointed pine boxes. Yes, my friends, I became an ampoholic.

I should probably mention that I have a degree in electrical engineering. I also spent six years in the U.S. Navy as an electrician's mate. So, truthfully, I know a thing or two about electrified contraptions. Something I noticed right away when I began eyeballing the schematics and innards of my old Fender amps was that they were ~~poorly~~ modestly engineered. I don't mean that in a bad way. I'm just saying that if *I* were asked to build a signal amplifying device for Rockwell, Rocketdyne, Honeywell, Lockheed Martin, North American Aviation, or any of them other high-tech companies back in those Space Race days, I'd probably have used more than a dozen parts, select components with tighter tolerances, and base the circuitry on something a bit more advanced than the 1930s RCA tube application manuals. People *did* make well engineered Hi-Fi audio amplifiers in those days. They're quite popular with audiophiles today. I've never played a guitar through my brother-in-law's McIntosh, but from what I understand it wouldn't sound all that good. Nor would his vinyl LP vibrations sound good amplified by my Lo-Fi 1956 Deluxe. But plug a Telecaster into that same Lo-Fi Deluxe and … well, you know.

Leo Fender's amps truly did evolve. He made them louder and increased the headroom as the '50s turned into the '60s. That's really what he was striving for. But those amps seemed to lose something magical. Musicians would soon begin connecting stomp boxes in the signal chain to downgrade these design and engineering advances. Leo Fender might have disliked that warm, creamy harmonic distortion that came with his earliest designs, but others dug it. Hell, Rock n' Roll was invented because of it. Don't get me wrong. I love my black-face amps, and I use them all the time. But if it's just me— alone—noodling about in the wee hours of the workday, I'm probably plugged into my narrow-panel Deluxe or brown Princeton. There's just something about those two low-power amps that makes me … happier?

The bottom line is that I'd love to figure out why I prefer Leo Fender's simpler, older designs over his magnum opus Music Man ones. So I took an aural journey of discovery and disguised it as the making of another Psychedelic Mooj album. Here's what I found:

- Fender amps sound good clean, great at the point of break up, and awesome fully cranked. For the brown and black-face amps, this awesomeness is inversely proportional to the size of the amp. For small brown and black-face amps, it can be mind-blowing. For the bigger brown and black-face amps, not so much. In some cases, it might even be nauseating. The tweeds, however, sound great no matter where that chickenhead is parked. And if you *can* crank them, you're going to be extremely happy.

- I love the juicy, well-rounded, smooth, rich distortion you get from a pair of 6V6s. But I also love the bold, firm, low end and prominent highs you get from a pair of 6L6s. Is one power tube pair combo better than the other? Nope. They're just different. In the end, we found ourselves adhering (mostly) to age-old custom of using mushy 6V6 amps for leads and the crunchy 6L6 amps for rhythm.

- Fender guitars and Fender amps made around the same time sound best together. It's a guitar pickup inductance/case candy cord capacitance/amp input stage impedance thing. Thus, I found that the 50's maple neck Telecasters and Stratocasters roar and rumble best in the tweeds. The slab-neck and L-Series Telecasters and Stratocasters growl and howl best in the brown amps. And, strangely, the gray bottom unwaxed pups of the mid-to late-60s sound best in the black-face amps. I know this is subjective, but I've played every guitar I have through every amp I have and this is true pretty much across the board.

- Les Pauls with humbuckers sound good in every amp. Les Pauls with touch sensitive P-90s sound even better in that same amp.

- The best sounding amp in my collection—without a doubt—is the 1959 Bandmaster. The 1960 Bandmaster, made just five months later, sounds completely different. Is it better or worse? That all depends. If I'm playing gut-wrenching blues, it's downright dreadful. But if I'm playing "Ram-Bunk-Shush," "Walk Don't Run," "Torquay," or "Moon of Manakoora," it's perfect.

- My style of playing (sloppy and choppy with lots of pick attack) means amps with solid-state rectifiers are less appealing to me. I truly love the spongy/squishy sag of a tube rectifier. I guess I'd never be a good jazz man.

- If someone ever made an amp with a Jensen P12R speaker, cathodyne PI, cathode-biased 6V6s, no negative feedback loop, and undersized Output Transformer (OT), it would be awesome. Oh wait! That's the 5E3 Deluxe!

- NOS tubes are a must.

- It's really all about the speakers, OT, tubes, PI, and tone stack location. They define the overall essence of an amp. Everything else is just icing on the cake.

'52 Tele Through a '56 Deluxe. That's a Brown Box Next to the Amp, Keeping Input Voltage at 110 V.

GUITARS AND AMPS

We used 14 amps and 15 guitars on *Naked and Dimed*. A little excessive? Probably. But if we didn't do it, who would? The guitars and amps are summarized below:

The Guitars

- 1952 Fender Telecaster (#5297)

- 1955 Fender Esquire (#09741)

- 1955 Gibson Les Paul (#59502)

- 1957 Fender Stratocaster (#15051)

- 1958 Danelectro/Spiegel UB-2 (#4088)

- 1963 Fender Precision Bass (#99112)

- 1963 Fender Stratocaster (#L23080)

- 1966 Fender Electric XII (#129297)

- 1968 Fender Telecaster Custom (#F250461)

- 1969 Fender Stratocaster (#266686)

- 1977 Fender Telecaster (#S728760)

- 1982 Gibson 30th Anniversary Les Paul (#A0040)

- 1983 G&L SC-2 (#G010570)

- 2007 Gibson Les Paul R9 (#971591)

- 2015 Newman 5-String (#5-0005)

The Amps

Narrow-Panel Tweed Era:

- 1956 Deluxe 5E3 (#D02606)
- 1956 Pro 5E5-B (#S00529)
- 1959 Bandmaster 5E7 (#S03639)
- 1963 Champ 5F1 (#C20209)

The Brown Era:

- 1960 Bandmaster 5G7 (#00484)
- 1961 Concert 6G12-A (#02947)
- 1961 Deluxe 6G3 (#D00668)
- 1963 Vibroverb 6G16 (#00574)
- 1963 Princeton 6G2 (#P05766)
- 1963 Reverb Unit 6G15 (#R03863)

The Black-Face Era:

- 1964 Princeton Reverb AB-764 (#A02543)
- 1964 Deluxe Reverb AB-763 (#A02231)
- 1965 Vibrolux Reverb AA-864 (#A02128)
- 1967 Super Reverb AB-763 (#A25441)

The Bottom End:

- 1967 Ampeg B-18-N (#051966) mounted atop B15 cabinet

We didn't use TV-front or wide-panel tweeds on *Naked and Dimed*. You'll hear those on *Naked and Dimed II*. I hope to one day have a complete set of Deluxes (from the Model 26 to the solid-state Robbie the Robot-looking thing) and talk my Moojmates into making another album where we'll use only Deluxes. Alas, if only we amused others as much as we amuse ourselves.

It was suggested by many wiser than us to use only one guitar for the whole album. Then each amp could truly be compared without introducing the tonal variances caused by the different guitars. We didn't do that because … well, that would have been boring. I know we'll get grief over this but I promise, we chose the right guitar for each amp.

The P'Mooj and Shane Matsumoto at SER Soundworks, 2019.

Recording The Amps

Shane Matsumoto is no stranger to the Psychedelic Mooj. He's produced, recorded, mixed, and mastered our last three albums. On *Analog Soup* and *Further than You Ever Knew* he captured our wah-wah laden, overdriven guitar attacks perfectly. There're tons of rhythm and lead guitar tracks interwoven around the thundering drum and bass tracks. For *Naked and Dimed,* he kept things simple. There's basically one rhythm track and one lead track. We wanted you to really hear each amp. These amps were made to be played and that's what we did. You'll wince when you hear how hard we pushed some of them. I was eternally grateful that we didn't smoke OTs or blow speakers during the sessions. That would have sucked.

Most of the amps were recorded in a small "closet" next to the control room. The guitar cord went through the wall. Richard Chavez and I played our guitar parts while lounging in the air-conditioned control room. Two mics were used for each amp. Shane reversed the polarity on the 2nd mic.

The Ampeg and Bandmasters were recorded in a large studio room. This was done before we decided on the protocol of using only the amp closest.

All the amps performed exceptionally well. I remember often thinking: "I wish I could use *that* amp for the whole album!" You have no idea how hard it was to stop using the '59 Bandmaster and move on to the next amp. The '56 Deluxe and '63 Princeton were also difficult to pull out of the amp closet. One amp actually *did* survive the eviction notice. The '65 Vibrolux Reverb remained inside the closet for three additional tracks. My '64 Deluxe Reverb, waiting patiently in the on deck circle, had to return another day.

This album took eight months to complete because we recorded only one or two guitar tracks per session. This was done to keep us honest (otherwise, I'd have been too tempted to keep using the same amp when that amp was sounding incredible—and many were).

A Research Project Cleverly Disguised as a Psychedelic Mooj Album.

Guitar and Amp Matrix

Guitar	Amp	Song
1955 Gibson Les Paul	1963 Fender Champ	*Steal My Heart* solos
1955 Fender Esquire	1963 Fender Champ	*Steal My Heart* solos (starting at 5:07)
1957 Fender Stratocaster	1963 Fender Princeton	*Knocking on Your Door* solos
1963 Fender Stratocaster	1963 Fender Reverb Unit/1963 Fender Princeton	*Nothing Can Be Found* solos
1977 Fender Telecaster	1964 Fender Princeton Reverb	*Dream within a Dream* solos
1963 Fender Stratocaster	1964 Fender Princeton Reverb	*Dream within a Dream* solo (2:29 to 2:41)
1955 Gibson Les Paul	1956 Fender Deluxe	*Horseshit Song* rhythm (double tracked)
1952 Fender Telecaster	1956 Fender Deluxe	*Who's Gonna Love Ya* & *Horseshit Song* solos
1957 Fender Stratocaster	1961 Fender Deluxe	*You Know* & *Begging for Mercy* rhythms
1969 Fender Stratocaster	1961 Fender Deluxe	*Nothing Can Be Found* rhythm
1983 G&L SC-2	1964 Fender Deluxe Reverb	*A Super Reverb & Deluxe Reverb* odd numbered solos
2007 Gibson Les Paul R9	1964 Fender Deluxe Reverb	*A Super Reverb & Deluxe Reverb* even numbered solos
1963 Fender Stratocaster	1963 Fender Vibroverb	*Steal My Heart* , *I Know*, and *We All Know* rhythms
2015 Newman 5-String	1965 Fender Vibrolux Reverb	*Last Goldtop Out of Kalamazoo* rhythm
1982 Gibson Les Paul (30th Anniv)	1965 Fender Vibrolux Reverb	*Last Goldtop out of Kalamazoo* solos
1966 Fender Electric XII	1965 Fender Vibrolux Reverb	*We All Know* solos
1968 Fender Telecaster Custom	1965 Fender Vibrolux Reverb	*Begging for Mercy* solos
1955 Fender Esquire	1956 Fender Pro	*I Know* solos
1955 Fender Esquire	1959 Fender Bandmaster	*Who's Gonna Love Ya* rhythm
1955 Gibson Les Paul	1959 Fender Bandmaster	*Knocking on Your Door* rhythm
1955 Gibson Les Paul	1960 Fender Bandmaster	*Dream within a Dream* rhythm
1958 Danelectro Spiegel UB-2	1961 Fender Concert	*Knox County Line*
1969 Fender Stratocaster	1967 Fender Super Reverb	*A Super Reverb & Deluxe Reverb* rhythm
1958 Danelectro Spiegel UB-2	1967 Ampeg B-18-N (on B15 Cab)	Bass on *Horseshit Song*
1963 Fender Precision Bass	1967 Ampeg B-18-N (on B15 Cab)	All other bass tracks

Richard Chavez in the Mooj Cave.

The Mooj Cave

Jamming in the Mooj Cave.

Sadly, the Mooj Cave no longer exists. For 10+ years it was my own personal Disneyland. It was my happiest place on earth. I ran a family business and had several warehouses. Some of those warehouses had unused office space. I took over one empty office to house my guitar and amp collection. It was in that room that my Moojmates and I jammed every weekend. Rick Obenshain left his drums set up in the room and Dave Hull kept his large Kustom rig parked against the wall. Richard Chavez never needed to bring a guitar amp because the room was filled with them. It was truly the ultimate place to rehearse and jam.

The greatest thing about the Mooj Cave was that it was only a three-minute walk from my office. Every afternoon I'd wander over there and choose a guitar and amp to play. My guys knew where to find me so I could be coaxed back during plant emergencies. Then at 5:00 p.m. something wonderful happened. The guys in the adjacent businesses went home. That's when the volume knob was spun clockwise. Most guys are afraid to "dime" their vintage amps. But, truthfully, they love to be played loud. If you don't, they'll die. (Well, the filter caps will certainly leak.)

Organizing the Mooj Cave before Recording Naked and Dimed.

Let's Make Another Album!

I remember calling Rick Obenshain and Richard Chavez and asking them if they would be interested in doing the *Naked and Dimed* album. "Hell yeah!" was their response. We'd been dormant for a while. We still jammed occasionally but it was usually just as a trio (Chavez or I played bass). This would be the first album without Dave Hull and he was going to be sorely missed.

I called Shane Matsumoto and we started organizing the project. I remember we were very ambitious in the early stages. I even considered videotaping the whole thing. That, however, would prove to be a budget killer.

We began recording *Naked and Dimed* on 11/19/2016. I knew it would take a long time to complete the album so it was my plan to have the CD, book, and website (with isolated tracks) come out at the same time. That didn't happen. The album was released on 8/07/2017, the website was finished on 5/5/2018, and the book never got written. But I'm writing it now! How did I get so side-tracked? Just life in general. Mainly, my business got sold and I had to vacate the Mooj Cave. Luckily, all the tracks had been recorded before I put everything in storage. I doubt we'd ever have completed the project if I didn't have the Mooj Cave to organize everything.

Rick Obenshain Recording Drum Tracks for Naked and Dimed.

THE GUITARS

Before we discuss the amplifiers, I'd like to introduce the guitars used on *Naked and Dimed*. They're all special. Some more than others.

My First Strat—"Kyrene."

Two of My Favorites: "Jenny" and "Shelby."

1983 G&L SC-2 "Blue Angel"

Do you still have your first electric guitar? Mine is this 1983 Viking Blue G&L SC-2. I bought it at Moody's Music in Garden Grove, CA in the Spring of 1983. It cost a whopping $425. That was a month's wages back then. I'd been saving for a used Stratocaster and was about halfway there. I went into Moody's to buy strings for an acoustic guitar my friend's sister had just sold me. This Viking Blue G&L SC-2 caught my eye. I paused to look at it. I'd heard about G&L. My friend Earl Gaugler was obsessed with Fender guitars (he was biding his time with a Lead II until he could afford a Stratocaster). Earl told me that Leo Fender had just started a new company called G&L. Earl read somewhere that Leo's new guitars were much better than his old ones. That sounded logical.

The salesman pounced on me before I could look away. He grabbed the SC-2, a cord, snapped on an amp, and handed me the guitar. I imagine I timidly sat on a stool and played the riffs for "Smoke on the Water," "Hair of the Dog" and "Heartbreaker." That's all I knew back then. I thanked the salesman and handed him back the guitar. This salesman was no fool. He knew a sucker when he saw one. He began wheeling and dealing. "I'll thrown in *this* and I'll thrown in *that*." I told him that I was saving my money to buy a used Stratocaster. "Why would you buy a used guitar when you can get a brand new *better* guitar for the same price?" he asked. Basically, the guy wouldn't take no for an answer. I surrendered my pocket money as a down payment. A "Sold" card was interweaved between the strings and the SC-2 was rehung on the wall. I regretted buying that SC-2 the moment I walked out of the store but I was too shy to return and ask for my money back.

No big deal. That SC-2 turned out to be a great guitar. And, truthfully, I'd buy plenty of "used" Stratocasters later in life.

One of the deals I got with my SC-2 was eight free lessons. I got to use my SC-2 for those lessons and then sadly hang it back on the wall when I was done. By August, the balance was paid and I brought "Blue Angel" home to meet mom and sister Debby. They were impressed. The neighbors? Not so much.

This SC-2 joined the navy with me in 1984. She was played loudly and proudly inside the Bachelor Enlisted Quarters of ITB Company 63 while I attended the prestigious Electrician Mate A-School in Great Lakes, IL. In those days, she was paired with a Roland Cube-20 solid state amplifier. That orange howler followed me everywhere I went in the navy. In fact, I still have it. I saw it on a shelf in my garage a few days ago. I wonder if it still works. Am I really too lazy the crawl down there and get it? I guess so.

My First Amp (I Wonder Who Signed that Navy Electrical Safety Tag?)

The Blue Angel was unceremoniously retired when my second guitar came along. I wouldn't see the SC-2 again for 30+ years. My mom obviously tossed her into the U-Haul my wife and I used to lug Uncle Joe's furniture to West LA after we got married because it followed me around everywhere we went after that. I discovered her long-unopened case under a pile of coats a few years ago. Naturally, I got teary-eyed when I gazed upon her again. She was, after all, my "first" love.

This SC-2 is actually a historic guitar. G&L's SC-1, SC-2, and SC-3 models introduced the world to Leo Fender's Magnetic Field Design (MFD) pickups. They utilized a ceramic bar magnet under each coil with soft iron adjustable pole pieces to transfer the magnetic field to the top of the pickup. Richard Smith in *Fender: The Sound Heard 'Round the World* claims these MFDs yield about twice the output per wind, making the pickup quieter and more powerful than earlier Fender single coil pickups. The SC-2 was also one of the first guitars to use Leo's new Dual Fulcrum Vibrato and a much better adaptation of his 3-bolt Tilt Neck idea.

I really wanted to use the Blue Angel on *Naked and Dimed* because, truthfully, I couldn't remember how she sounded. I only had vague memories of her being harsh through the little Cube-20. I don't want to ruin any surprises but you'll be blown away (like I was) when you hear her through the 1964 Deluxe Reverb. Leo, I must say, your MFD pups really *do* sound awesome!

MFD Pickups and Dual Fulcrum Vibrato—Two of Leo Fender's Last Innovations.

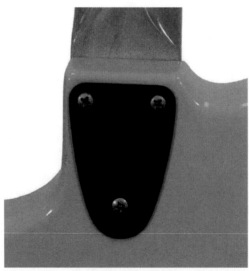

The 3-Bolt Tilt Neck Leo Wanted ... Better than the One Used by FMI from 1971-1979

1982 Les Paul "Pride and Joy"

I could only dream about owning a genuine Les Paul when I was a kid. Even neck-repaired clown 'bursts commanded big bucks in the weekly *Recycler*. No one I knew had a real one. Then again, no one I knew had a real Stratocaster either.

I remember seeing a brand new 30th Anniversary Les Paul on the wall at Moody's Music in the summer of 1983. It got my attention the moment I walked into the store. It was the most beautiful thing I had ever seen. Alas, there was no touching a gem like that when all you could do was put a student model G&L on layaway.

A year later I was stationed in Orlando, FL just about to begin Naval Nuclear Power School. I'd saved $400 and decided it was time to finally buy that used Stratocaster I had always wanted. I bummed a ride to the local music store and—behold—there upon the wall was a 30th Anniversary Les Paul! I shoved my $400 into the salesman's palm for a down payment.

The next day I stood in line at the Orlando Navy Credit Union and asked for a $500 loan to pay off the balance. You'd have thought I was applying for a million bucks the way they gawked at me. Finally, someone there suggested that I cross out "I need the money for a guitar" and put "I need the money for a car" on my application. That worked. I wasn't old enough to legally drink yet but I owned a genuine Les Paul goldtop. I named her "Pride and Joy" because that was the first song I learned to play on her.

This Les Paul has been my friend and companion for over 35 years now. Like many, I sometimes see and buy irresistible R9 'bursts, but truthfully this old gal sounds better than any of them. The Tim Shaw pups on this rare LP are amazing.

Because she was my only Les Paul for 30+ years, she's been used on every Psychedelic Mooj album. She's also been used in countless shows.

These 30th Anniversary models were among the last guitars made in the Kalamazoo factory and considered by many to be Gibson's first attempt at making "historic reissues." They truly were unique in that they were made by some of the same people who built the originals on the original machinery and tooling.

These days, "Pride and Joy" is modified for slide. The Tune-O-Matic is raised, the pups are raised, and she's outfitted with very heavy strings.

"Pride and Joy" Set Up for Slide.

Has Anyone Ever Been Able to Make Sense of These 30th Anniv. Serial Numbers?

1977 Telecaster "Christine"

I have many "special" guitars but Christine gets to be buried with me. We've sailed around the world three times and grown old together.

Oddly, as orthodox as I am about keeping guitars as original as possible, the only thing still 1977 about Christine is her neck and hardware, *but* I still have her original parts. Whether or not I could actually find them is a different story. I guess, logically, I could put her back together again. Then she'd be worth a whopping $2,050 (value of a 1977 Telecaster in 2019). Or, perhaps, I'll just leave her the way she's been for the last 34 years because that's the Christine I've known and loved for 60-percent of my life. I'm guessing I'll just leave her be.

How did we meet? Thanks for asking. It was a warm summer day in 1985. I was stationed at the Knolls Atomic Power Laboratory in Ballston Spa, NY. My roommate and I decided to drive down to that happening hotspot known as Schenectady, NY. We saw Drome Sound and stopped in to take a peek. They had a whole wall of used Fenders for sale. I adopted a $400 Telecaster[1]. She would later be named "Christine" after I finished reading the Stephen King book with the same name.

Originally, Christine had a yellowed, cream colored ash body and black, three-ply pickguard. She didn't remain like that for long. The next time I was at Drome Sound I bought a 'Paul C' Telecaster Custom body. If memory serves me right, I paid $250 for it. My $400 Tele was now a $650 "better looking but worth half" Telecaster.

I didn't stop there. A month later, I swapped the neck pickup for a '50s Seymour Duncan (I think the original died). The new pickup sounded so good that I decided to screw a Seymour Duncan into the bridge plate. Drome didn't have any Duncan '50s Tele bridge pups so I took home a Duncan '60s staggered pole piece one instead.

Six months later I reported aboard the *USS Enterprise* (CVN 65). She was steaming off the coast of Subic Bay, Philippines. I was told to bring only my sea bag and garment bag. I took Christine, too. I suffered for that flagrant act of disobedience. I had nowhere to stow Christine. We slept together until someone showed me a void, located deep within the bowels of the ship were others hid their contraband. Every night I'd crawl down into that dark and dank space to spend a little time with my Christine.

---

[1] I cannot remember why I chose to buy this used Telecaster over a Stratocaster. In those days, both were about $400. I had gone there specifically to find a Stratocaster.

Next, you'll read about my second Telecaster. That one was too valuable to be kept on a warship so she resided in my mom's guestroom closet for many years. Christine would remain with me in the fleet for my entire enlistment. We'd jam together hours a day while at sea, play numerous shows with the Big E Band, and fight in the largest naval battle fought since World War II. Christine earned three sea service ribbons and a pickguard full of expedition medals. She could join the American Legion if she wanted to.

Christine was my main axe in college after the navy. She lived under the hatchback of my Honda CRX as I drove around San Luis Obispo County looking for jams. We took the stage together many times with the Low Rent Blues Band. Those were great days for a young man and his guitar.

The Psychedelic Mooj Laying Down Some Low-Down Blues, 2007.

Christine's Original Body

These Old Receipts From Drome are Still in Christine's Case.

1952 Telecaster "Jenny"

The *USS Enterprise* returned to Alameda in the summer of 1986. I'd saved a whopping $2,000 during the cruise and planned to use it for a vintage Stratocaster. I'd read and re-read Andre Duchossoir's *The Fender Stratocaster* a thousand times while at sea. I was as knowledgeable as any 22-year-old kid could be about old Stratocasters. As soon as the Big E's mooring lines were secured, I was off on my search. My steaming mates (and fellow guitar players) Richard Hordyke, John Hutchings, and Rob Gargano joined me on my hunt. Strangely, all we could find were CBS-era Mustangs and 3-bolt naturals. Could it be that there wasn't *one* vintage Stratocaster in the entire Bay Area for sale? It sure seemed that way.

Then we stumbled into Real Guitars in San Francisco. Chris Cobb had just opened the place. I asked him if he had any Pre-CBS Stratocasters. I expected the usual sad-faced reply. Instead, Chris pointed to the wall. Two green 'guards[2] hung there. Either could be had for $1,800. I played both, liked one better than the other, and pulled out my wallet. Chris's eyes bulged out. "I didn't realize you were a serious buyer," he said. (I was just a kid, remember.) Then Chris said something magical: "If you're interested, I just got in a 1952 Telecaster. However, someone's on his way in to ..." I didn't let him finish. "Bring it out!" I said.

It was love at first sight. I plugged her in and that was it—she *had* to be mine. The hang tag said $2,500. My wallet had a bit under $2,000. My steaming mates collected what they had, but we still came up short. Maybe Chris Cobb had to pay his rent or something because that was close enough to make her mine. I returned the next day (luckily it was a payday) and gave him the balance. I left the store doing my best not to look too conspicuous carrying the poodle case. A few years later that same guitar would be worth twice as much and I'd never be able to ethically afford one again. It was truly one of those "right place, right time" sort of things.

I kept Jenny with me during the dreaded dry dock days of late 1986 and early 1987. She was perilously stashed inside my Hunter's Point barracks locker. Our room was jam central back then. Every guitar player in the building gathered there nightly, and brought along an offering of beer. Those paint scraping days sucked but the evenings sure were fun.

I wisely took Jenny home before moving back on the ship. Then I didn't see her again unless I was home on leave. She remained with my mom while I was in the navy. She also stayed with mom while I was in college.

---

[2] I don't think they were called green 'guards back then. At least I never used that term. Maybe the nitrocellulose pickguards hadn't really turned "green" yet?

It's hard to imagine every time I hold Jenny that I'm holding something so historic. She's one of the first production solid body guitars ever made. She's old growth swamp ash and got those warm, round, brass saddles. I was told Jenny was a 1952 Telecaster when I bought her, but I never took her neck off. Over the years, I began to think she was more likely a 1953 Telecaster because of her serial number (# 5297) and the fact that she came in a poodle case. But she had slot-head screws and was wired with the original blended circuit. I finally learned the truth when Reed Munns took her apart in the summer of 2015 for a much-needed re-fret. Jenny's neck was made by Tadeo Gomez on 5/23/52 and the body was carved by Charlie Davis on 5/19/52.

Me and Jenny, Hunter's Point Dry Dock, 1986

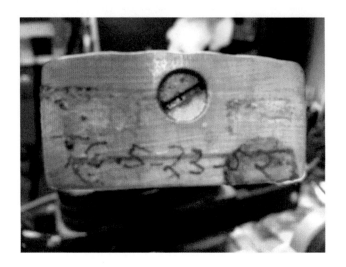

Tadio Gomez Carved Jenny's Neck on 5-23-52.

Charlie Davis Carved Jenny's Body on 5-19-52.

I Know of Only One Other 1952 Telecaster with a Higher Serial Number.

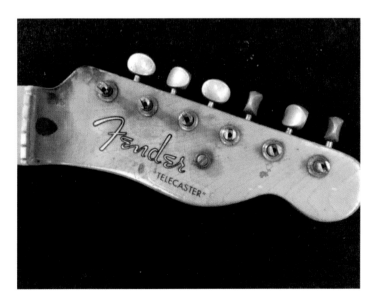

She Must Have Played a Lot of Honky Tonks.

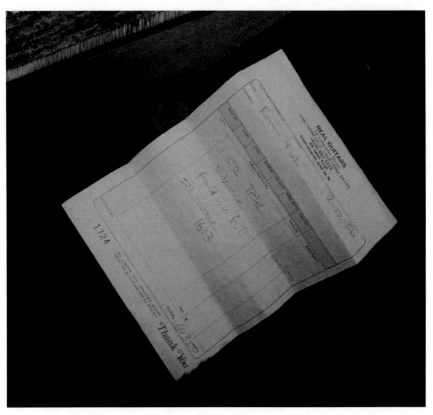

I Still Have the Receipt for Jenny in the Poodle Case.

1957 Stratocaster "Kyrene"

After buying Jenny I was a regular in Real Guitars. They yelled out my name when I walked in, just like they did for Norm at Cheers. I kept hoping to see a maple neck Stratocaster on the wall. I wouldn't be able to afford it, but I'd at least I'd get to play it.

The *USS Enterprise* got underway again in early 1988. I made my second cruise. I saved about $2,000 again. Maybe—just maybe—I'd return to San Francisco and find that old Stratocaster. Guess what? When I walked into Real Guitars in the fall of 1988, they had *two* 1957 Stratocasters on the wall! One was a shell pink re-fin and the other was a beat to hell all original hardtail. I could have either for $2,000. I bought the hardtail. It seemed to be calling my name.

After the 1988 cruise, I rented a house in Dublin, CA with three of my shipmates. That was one of the happiest times of my life. My future wife and I began our storybook romance and I got to play Kyrene every day.

Then began the dreaded workups, prepping for my last cruise. We were at sea more than in port and it was pointless to pay rent on a house we never slept in. I drove south to my dad's home in San Pedro and left Kyrene with him. I'd retrieve her in the spring of 1990 after I got out of the navy and went to college.

I used Kyrene in some Low Rent Blues shows, but knew better than to gig too blatantly with her. Those were the days before "relics" so if you were seen on stage with a lacquer-less neck, it was probably the real thing.

Kyrene was never used in the studio before *Naked and Dimed*. That's because she was so "player vintage" by 2006 that she couldn't be played anymore. Her frets were rutted like the old Santa Fe Trail and I had to wiggle the cord and smack the single-ply 'guard to get her to wake up. I finally took her to Reed Munns in Tucson for a much-needed re-fret. He also replaced the jack, lubed and cleaned the pots, and corrected the loose cloth-covered wiring mishaps. She was alive again. I wasn't sure who was happier, me or Kyrene.

I was told Kyrene was a 1957 Stratocaster when I bought her. But like Jenny, I never took off her neck. Over the years, I began to suspect that she was really a 1956 Stratocaster because of her serial number (#15051), round string tree, and extremely deep V-neck. I finally learned the truth when Reed Munns took her apart for the 2015 re-fret. She had 1/57 penciled on her neck heel (Forrest White) and the body was dated 10/56. Oddly, there are many 1-57 Strats out there with 10/56 bodies. The Fender Factory must have been shut down for the holidays.

Filming "Sterling Sea of Blue" Video

College Life ...

*Recording Our Second Album. "Pride and Joy," "Christine," "Belle," and "Jenny." Belle,
the Ocean Turquoise Strat is a '57 Re-Issue.*

Our Second Album. It's So Rare that Even I Don't Have a Copy ...

Two 1963 Oddball Danelectros

I won't lie. Life aboard an aircraft carrier could suck at times. One such time was when a new master chief showed up, took one look around, and proclaimed: "Listen up, you scumbags! This is a warship not a college dormitory! Get all this [crap] out of berthing—now!" I think he was mostly talking about bikes, stereos, and surfboards, but his unauthorized gear also included guitars. Poor Christine had to go. I wasn't sure how I was going to cope with being at sea without her. My solution was to smuggle a small guitar aboard and hide it between the dungarees in my steaming locker. A 1963 Danelectro Pro-1 did the trick. I bought it at Real Guitars for $250.

I used to have a website (maybe I still do) where I showed pictures of my guitars. Believe it or not, this Pro-1 garnered the most attention. People would beg me to sell it to them. They didn't care about the black 'guard Tele or hardtail Strat. This ¾ scale Flintstone-age looking oddity was all anyone wanted. These were only made for a year and are quite rare.

Hey! I just realized that I didn't use "Danno" on *Naked and Dimed*. I probably shouldn't have mentioned her. Oh well. I'm the author/editor/publisher so I guess I can do anything I want, right?

I did use Danno on the previous Psychedelic Mooj album. That's her sliding around on *Further than You Ever Knew*'s "What's Going On?" Danno is about the twangiest-sounding guitar you'll ever meet.

Since I mentioned Danno, I might as well mention "The Rumbler." I bought him at Real Guitars in either 1987 or 1988. I thought he was just the usual run-of-the-mill "Longhorn" that SRV and others were playing in those days. I never really noticed the 31 frets. It was both guitar and mandolin in one. I brought both Danelectros home before the 1988 cruise. They were wedged beside Jenny's poodle case in my mom's closest. Thank you, mom, for not selling them.

Real Life Begins

I got out of the navy in 1990 and my vintage guitar buying days ended abruptly. Actually, buying *anything* ended abruptly. I was officially a starving student. While in college, I jammed with anyone who'd allow me through their student apartment door. I was in peak form back then. I seriously thought about making a go of it, but owed it to my future wife and children not to make them suffer alongside me. I made a deal with myself. I'd finish college, become an engineer, make a decent living, and *then* become a bluesman. So, that's what I did. I only had to wait fifteen years to live my dream.

Life changed after college. I got married, moved to LA, and became a graduate student. I was a model citizen (so they say). In 1995, I was done with all my schooling. My wife, first born, and I moved to Maryland. I was finally—at the age of 32—a working man.

The years just flew by. We added three more children to the family. From 1995 until 2002 I rarely if ever played guitar. I was totally focused on my family and work.

The Psychedelic Mooj

We moved to Phoenix in 2002 to help run a family business. I now had a bit of downtime as I waited for equipment and machinery to arrive. I pulled the '82 goldtop and '77 Telecaster out from under the bed and took them to work. I was finally playing guitar again.

Richard Chavez, Tracy Miranda-Binkley, Dave Hull and I formed a band called The Psychedelic Mooj in early 2005. We all had one thing in common: we were older, had given up music to raise families, and now wanted just to play music again. We soon got bored jamming in a warehouse and began playing the local bar circuit and making albums.

My Wife and Kids Visit Me at the New Office. Where's the Youngest? Oh, He Must be Out Back Working. Not Much Going On (Yet) but I was Starting to Play Guitar Again!

The Psychedelic Mooj ... Melting Minds One Show at a Time.

Using Corona Guitars Through Fullerton Amps

On a lark, I bought a 2006 Fender Custom Shop Fiesta Red '56 Stratocaster Relic at Guitar Center. It looked abandoned on the "used" wall. I made a low-ball offer and was astonished when the salesman came running back and said the manager accepted it. It was one of those sad/happy moments.

Although I loved the look and feel of this guitar, it didn't sound right through my Clyde/OCD/Deluxe Reverb Re-issue set up. By then, I had perfected my *Analog Soup* sound and this wasn't it. The Fiesta Red beauty was hung in a display case in my living room.

Then I started exploring vintage amps. I realized right away that my '57 Vintage Re-issue Strats (I had two, a 2003 Ocean Turquoise one named "Belle" and a 2008 Surf Green one named "Magpie") sounded horrible in the old amps. They were brittle and harsh. I was curious how the 2006 Custom Shop Relic might sound in a vintage amp. It came out of the display case and actually sounded pretty good in everything. So good, in fact, that it never went back into the display case again. Could it be that some guitars and amps weren't compatible? I was beginning to find out that was true.

My Mid-Life Crisis

I read Dave Hunter's *365 Guitars, Amps & Affects You Must Play* in 2013 and took the challenge (well, at least until my wife caught on). These days, that list has been narrowed down considerably. *Naked and Dimed* was made using guitars and amps on that so-called bucket list. I guess I could have called the album *7-Percent of the Dave Hunter's Guitars, Amps & Affects You Must Play*.

Let me now show you some of the guitars I added to my collection in the second half of my life …

Our First Album

The Fiesta Red Strat Makes a Rare Appearance.

1963 Stratocaster "Shelby"

In the Fall of 2013 Mark Lovett sold me his 1963 Candy Apple Red Stratocaster. The neck was stamped Dec, 1963. That was the month and year I was born. There was a big difference between the vintage stuff I bought as a sailor 23 years before and this particular instrument. The gear I collected in my navy days was "player vintage" and bought long before the feeding frenzy of the 1990s. This 1963 Stratocaster was a museum piece, and had just graced Pages 100 and 101 of Dave Hunter's *The Fender Stratocaster, The Life & Times of the World's Greatest Guitar & Its Players*. It had a distinguished pedigree. For my 50th birthday, my wife told me to add my name to the bottom of that list.

This 1963 Strat arrived just as we began recording *Further than you Ever Knew*. I was only going to delicately play her once, deftly wipe her off, and put her away. But she sounded so damn good that I kept bringing her back to the studio. In the end, she was used on "GT350," "Sometimes it Happens that Way," "Blood in the Snow" and the title track, "Further than You Ever Knew." On the title track you can hear how rich and dark she sounds compared to the brighter '57 Re-issue. Both are playing in separate channels in the outro.

"Shelby" and "Magpie" at SER Studios. They were Used for Most of the Tracks on Further than You Ever Knew. *You Can Totally Hear the Difference Between the Two. The '63 Strat is Dark and Commanding. The '57 Vintage Re-Issue is Bright and Twangy.*

Chavez Drives "Shelby" like a Mack Truck on the Rhythm Tracks of "I Know" and "Steal My Heart."

1955 Les Paul "The Stumbler"

I bought this '55 "all gold" Les Paul from Harvey Moltz. It's the best sounding Les Paul I've ever heard. You think I'm fooling? Have a listen to *Naked and Dimed*. It's used on 38-percent of the tracks.

Here's how I came upon this guitar. My wife and I were in Tucson to pick up our eldest daughter. She was finishing finals at the University of Arizona. We had about an hour to kill so I talked my wife into going to Rainbow Guitars. I had never been there but my Moojmate Chavez loved the place. He bought all his Fender and Gibson Custom Shop guitars there.

I couldn't believe my eyes when I poked my head inside this humble-looking (from the outside) guitar emporium. It was guitar nirvana. I ran from one Fender Custom Shop instrument to another. My wife decided to wait in the car. Soon, I was getting texts: "Where are you?" "It's time to go." "What are you doing?"

Where was I? I was with Harvey Moltz! He came out of his office and we started talking. The next thing I knew, I was in his office where I could gaze upon a wall of vintage axes. One guitar caught my eye immediately. It was a 1955 blonde Esquire. It had flat pole pieces hidden under the ashtray. I already had a black 'guard Tele so I figured it wouldn't make any sense to fall in love with an Esquire. Spoiler alert: an Esquire is a totally different beast than a Telecaster!

Then Harvey showed me his all gold 1955 Les Paul. We took it to the amp room and he let me play it. *Wham!* I love P-90s and McCarthy (i.e., stop-tail) bridges. I'm one of those guys who thinks the Tune-O-Matic is a horrific tone sucker. This '55 Goldtop was incredible. I had never experienced Lester enlightenment like that before. "Is … this … for sale?" I asked. Harvey said no. Or maybe he said yes. I can't remember. It was all a blur after that. Harvey told my wife a few years later that people always ask him how much guitars are but never actually buy them. He was stunned when I agreed to buy the Lester. I guess my wife was, too.

All Gold 5 9502. Les Pauls Made a Few Weeks Later Would Have the Tune-O-Matic Added.

Rainbow Guitars in Tucson.

Reed Munns and the Gang in Tucson are the Only Ones I'll Trust with my Vintage Guitars.

Chavez Laying Down the Rhythm Track for "Dream Within A Dream" with the '55 LP. It was the Only Guitar that Could Get the '60 Bandmaster to Breakup at a Reasonable Volume. We Almost "Cheated" and Used that Klon (but we didn't).

1955 Esquire "Angela"

You knew I'd buy Harvey's 1955 Esquire, too. Every time I saw "Angela" (the name was engraved on the bridge cover), she'd call out to me. I made the mistake of playing her once. Then she haunted me. Finally, I could stand it no longer and brought her home.

There's a reason black 'guard Teles are lusted after more than white 'guard Teles. It's all about that bridge pickup. Leo Fender—ever the tinkerer—always took something perfect and refined it so that it wasn't so perfect anymore. The Tele bridge pup is a good example. Nothing sounds better than the flat pole piece pups that were put in the earliest Telecasters. In 1955 Fender began installing staggered height pole pieces in the bridge plates to give the Telecaster a more balanced and even sound. Well, naturally, gone was a bit of that Tele magic. So if you can find an early '55 Tele or Esquire with flat pole pieces, you just got a black 'guard for the price of a white 'guard. (A few years later Fender would do even more harm to the Telecaster when they began sending top-loaders out the door—but I won't go there.)

This '55 one-pup-wonder has way more bite and sustain than my '52 Tele. Perhaps the lone pickup was a too hot to be adequately matched with another in a Telecaster. Or, maybe the fact that there's no neck coil magnetic flux slowing down the string vibrations make her so incredibly powerful. Whatever it is, this Esquire cuts through the mix like a rip-saw. She was used on many *Naked and Dimed* songs. You'll definitely hear the difference between her and Jenny on the album.

Flat Pole Pieces Make All the Difference.

1963 Precision Bass "Sinbad"

What came first, the 1963 P-Bass or the 1967 Ampeg B-18-N Portaflex? One thing is certain: when I had one, I had to have the other.

I named this badass bass "Sinbad" because he kind of looked like my childhood dog. Sinbad was a German Shepherd/Collie mix.

Sadly, Psychedelic Mooj bassist Dave Hull never got to play Sinbad. He would have loved it. He would have also loved the Ampeg B-18-N. He often talked about the Ampegs of his youth. When he and I first started talking about making the all vintage instrument album, he didn't really like the idea of using a vintage bass amp. He was politely telling me that my tweed Bassman sucked. My Bassman was old, but it wasn't *that* old. It was a 1991 Re-issue. I picked it up somewhere for $500. Dave normally played through a big Kustom rig, but it went down during a busy period and he had to use my Re-issue Bassman. By the time the Kustom was back in service, the Bassman wasn't. It was rackety and cone-torn. I bought replacement P10R speakers for it and had John Markovich install them and tighten things up. Later John joked, "don't play bass through this anymore."

Anyway, I've digressed. Now back to Sinbad. When Richard, Rick, and I finally moved forward to make *Naked and Dimed*, I thought it would be cool to use an old bass on the project. But I didn't have one or really know much about basses. I did my research and learned everything I could about vintage P-Basses and J-Basses. Then I started looking, hoping to find something really cool. I did! It was hanging on Harvey Moltz's wall. I was there, trying to talk him out of the narrow-panel Super under his desk (it's still there by the way). "Hey, when did you get *that?*" I asked, suddenly seeing this black-beauty on the wall. Harvey said he'd had it for 4 years. "Really?" I had never noticed. Well, it came home with me.

I know P-Basses didn't leave the Fender factory in 1963 with matching headstocks. Some J-Basses did. Was this bass sent back to Fender in the mid-60s and re-finned? That's what I tell people. More than likely Earl Scheib did it for $29.95. Who really knows?

I had never played much bass before 2016. Then all of a sudden, I was playing bass for hours a day. I even wheeled the B-18-N out of the Mooj Cave and into to my office. I wasn't getting work done anymore. The guys in the back were probably wondering what all that thumping was about. I'd like to find a J-Bass from that same era and see what the differences between the two are. Maybe for *Naked and Dimed II?*

Relec'd The Old Fashioned Way

1969 Stratocaster "Charlotte"

Remember that black maple cap Stratocaster Hendrix used on the *Band of Gypsies* album? How about the Strat David Gilmore used on *Live at Pompeii*? Was there ever a cooler looking Stratocaster? I think not. Here's how I got mine.

Harvey Moltz had a big headstock Stratocaster on his wall the day we met. He told me it was a 69/70 ('69 neck on a '70 body). He'd had it for 20+ years, but hadn't played it in a long time because it had some wiring issue. I never asked for details because I was too busy ogling the Esquire. A year or two later I was standing at Harvey's desk and my jaw dropped. How was it possible that I had looked at that Stratocaster a dozen times and never realized it had a maple cap neck? Harvey said he'd give me a great deal on it. (Harvey tells me that a lot.) I didn't buy it that day, but soon I was obsessed. It would float around in my dreams (not the guitar, just the neck). Then one night I sat up in bed. "Hey! If I found a black '69 body to go with that '69 maple cap neck—it'd be a real '69 Strat—right?"

I called up Eddie Vegas. He had both a black and Olympic White '69 body (both re-fins). I told him to send the black one.

Reed Munns put Charlotte together and fixed the wiring issue. I swear it's one of the best sounding and playing Stratocasters I have.

The Neighbors Are Gone. It's Gonna Get Loud!

1958 Spiegel UB-2 "Nez"

I dig Danelectros. Who doesn't? The amount of tone you get from that cheesy lipstick pickup, Masonite body, and stiff metal-rod poplar neck is incredible. It took me years to finally find this single cutaway 6-string bass. I bought it from Retrofret Vintage Guitars in NYC. This bass/guitar is one of my favorite instruments. When I finally had it in the Mooj Cave, I played it for hours a day.

I learned right away not to play this guy too rough. The strings vibrate out of the bridge slots if you're not careful.

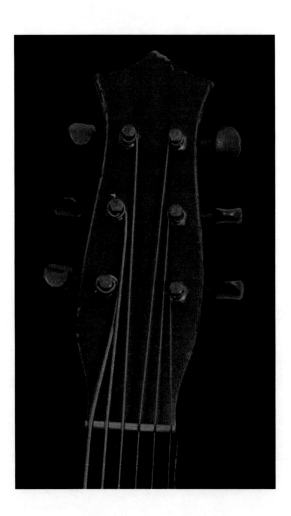

1966 Electric XII "Brutus"

I always wanted one of these hockey stick Electric XIIs. These are rare, but not scarce. I decided to hunt for a cool custom-colored one. A big name vintage store in Chicago had an Olympic White one. I was just about to pull the trigger when Craig Brody listed this incredible Ice Blue Metallic beauty. I jumped on the phone. Craig told me that it was probably already sold. "To whom!" I demanded (in a nice voice). Craig only mentioned that the potential buyer lived in a faraway place and was having trouble getting the money together. I called him a day later and he still hadn't heard from the guy. Sorry whoever you were, I jumped your claim.

These Electric XIIs were introduced in the ebb of the electric 12-string era so they weren't sold for very long. Luckily, someone famous built a Stairway to Heaven with one so they're somewhat appreciated. I love mine. I write strange songs with it. These songs don't go anywhere yet, but I'm still young.

I wasn't even thinking about using this Electric XII on the *Naked and Dimed* until speaking with Gil Southworth Jr. For some reason we were talking about Electric XIIs that day. I told him, "You know what, I still haven't put the coffin lid on the *Naked and Dimed* recording sessions. I'm going to bring my Electric XXII to the studio and use it!" So I did.

Recording Fills and Solos on "We All Know."

1968 Telecaster Custom "Kate"

I have numerous Fender stringed instruments and only a handful have rosewood fingerboards. The rest have maple necks. Of those maple necks, 3 are actually maple caps (i.e., instead of a rosewood fingerboard, a maple board was used).

I love maple caps. What's the difference between a one piece maple neck and maple cap? The maple caps have something magical about them. I can't even really describe it. They seem firmer and more battleworthy. You never know, you might have to El Kabong someone at the Palomino one night and you'd rather do it with a maple cap than a '50s neck. Just saying.

I bought this '68 Lake Placid Blue Telecaster Custom from Brian Fischer in 2015. It was re-finned by Gord Miller. It was originally black but someone did something awful to the finish. People do that I guess. Everything else on this guitar was original, except for the neck pickup. I found the correct one (green and white cloth wire) and had it installed by Reed Munns when he did a re-fret. This is without a doubt one of the best sounding and playing Telecasters in my collection.

2007 Les Paul R9 "Ruby"

I admit there are times I wish I had a "real" 1959 Les Paul. But I'd rather have a house. I have lots of Facebook friends who have genuine 'bursts. If any lived nearby, I'd have invited them down to play their precious lute on the album. Let me know if any of you want in on *Naked and Dimed II*.

I've only played one true vintage 58/59/60 Les Paul. It was at Real Guitars in 1988. They had it in on consignment. I still remember it in vivid detail. It was more of a plain top than a 'burst and it had the footprint of a jettisoned Bigsby. How did it sound? Well, great of course. How much was it? $6,000. I might be able to save $2,000 on a six-month cruise, but not three times that. That was the closest I ever came to buying one—and it wasn't even close.

I bought "Ruby" on Reverb in 2015. It was basically love at first sight. Every once in a while I'd see the perfect cherry 'burst and this time the price was right. The Burstbuckers on Ruby sound great. In the Mooj Cave, this was usually Chavez's go-to guitar. Hopefully it's a good representation of how a real 1959 with PAFs would sound.

"Ruby" was Tom Murphy Aged.

2015 Newman 5-String "Tuli"

I've always been a big proponent of alternate tunings. My '82 Les Paul has spent most of its life in either Open E or Open D. I've also kept at least one of my Telecasters in Open G. About three years ago, I removed the low E string (theoretically that would be the D) on Christine. Maybe, just maybe, it was because I was now using tweed amps. Could it be that all those years of being a Keith Richards devotee was finally paying off? I think so.

I've been Facebook friends with Jeff Smith for a many years. Jeff keeps Ted Newman's legacy alive by continuing to build Ted's legendary guitars. I called him one day when I saw he was building a TV Yellow 5-string. "I want that guitar!" I told him. "Yours!" he said.

The 5-string "Tuli" model was made from a light piece of swamp ash and has a hard ash neck with curly maple fretboard. Ted Newman Jones passed away on July 1, 2016. This guitar was in progress of being made and wasn't completed until September. This was the first guitar I ever had built just for me. The EMG H4 and H4A passive pickups were chosen for the 5-string models by Ted. The bridge was also custom milled from a single piece of chrome-dipped aircraft grade aluminum.

I'll be honest. I was a bit leery about using EMG pickups. I knew traditional 6 pole pups wouldn't work with 5 strings, so I trusted Ted Newman's judgement. Man, was I happy when I first played this guitar. I plugged it into the Champ that sits next to my desk. I knew then that this was one hell of an incredible guitar.

The day the 1965 Vibrolux Reverb arrived I just so happened to still have the Newman in my office. Once I had the Vibrolux Reverb powered up, the Newman was plugged into it. I was floored. I had originally intended to use the Newman through a tweed Pro on *Naked and Dimed*. After hearing it through the Vibrolux Reverb, I knew I had found the perfect pairing.

Thank you, Jeff Smith. This is one of the best guitars I have—and it's named after me!

Jeff Smith and Me with the Newman "Tuli" Model.

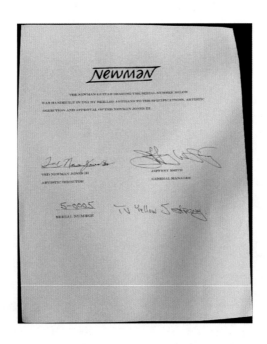

THE AMPS

I mentioned earlier that I've known my guitars for a long time. The vintage amps, however, have only been in my life for a few years. I've gotten to know them, but not as intimately as the guitars. In truth, *Naked and Dimed* was done so that I *could* get to know them better.

Before we proceed, I should probably point out that I'm not going to get too technical here. Part of me wants to show off my electrical engineering expertise; but, truthfully, there're so many other resources out there that delve into the intricacies of tone stacks, rectifiers, phase inverters, preamps, coupling caps, carbon composite resistors, output transformers, and all that happy stuff. I began this project by studying schematics, circling things, and even contemplated running an O-Scope at various points. Then I realized one can't quantify feelings. Perhaps, it would just be better to record the amps, listen, and hear how some (or all) of these component differences combine to make each amp unique and special. It turns out that even little changes in the evolving circuits made for huge differences. I didn't really notice how profound these differences were until I listened to the mastered tracks of *Naked and Dimed*.

Dialed In

I don't really mess with tone controls much while on stage or in the studio. I usually just set everything to 5 and leave it. That's what I did on *Naked and Dimed*. Volumes, however, started near the top and were slowly backed down while I searched for the "best-sounding" place as heard through the microphones and console. More than likely, this volume was slightly above the sweet spot (i.e., the point of break up). If the amp had reverb, I set it at 4 or 5. If vibrato was used, both speed and intensity were set to 5. I will indicate where I deviated from any of the above settings when discussing the individual amps in the recording section.

Speaker Configuration

One thing that might not be too well perceived on *Naked and Dimed* is how speaker configuration affects the overall experience of an amplifier. In the Mooj Cave, I could stand in front of the amp and feel the air gust past me. The recording process removed that sensual awareness. My opinion (if you want it) is that I like the sound and feel of 2x10 combo amps best.

4x10 1961 Concert

2x10 1963 Vibroverb

Using Tube Charts to Date Fender Amps

Most of you probably know this, but just in case you don't I'll add this bit of information here. Fender stamped two letters on the tube chart of every amplifier leaving the factory after 1953. The first letter represents the year and the second letter represents the month. For example, an amp made in 1961-February would be stamped "KB."

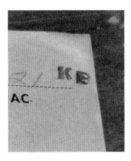

	Jan	Feb	Mar	Apr	May	Jun	Jul	Aug	Sep	Oct	Nov	Dec
1953	CA	CB	CC	CD	CE	CF	CG	CH	CI	CJ	CK	CL
1954	DA	DB	DC	DD	DE	DF	DG	DH	DI	DJ	DK	DL
1955	EA	EB	EC	ED	EE	EF	EG	EH	EI	EJ	EK	EL
1956	FA	FB	FC	FD	FE	FF	FG	FH	FI	FJ	FK	FL
1957	GA	GB	GC	GD	GE	GF	GG	GH	GI	GJ	GK	GL
1958	HA	HB	HC	HD	HE	HF	HG	HH	HI	HJ	HK	HL
1959	IA	IB	IC	ID	IE	IF	IG	IH	II	IJ	IK	IL
1960	JA	JB	JC	JD	JE	JF	JG	JH	JI	JJ	JK	JL
1961	KA	KB	KC	KD	KE	KF	KG	KH	KI	KJ	KK	KL
1962	LA	LB	LC	LD	LE	LF	LG	LH	LI	LJ	LK	LL
1963	MA	MB	MC	MD	ME	MF	MG	MH	MI	MJ	MK	ML
1964	NA	NB	NC	ND	NE	NF	NG	NH	NI	NJ	NK	NL
1965	OA	OB	OC	OD	OE	OF	OG	OH	OI	OJ	OK	OL
1966	PA	PB	PC	PD	PE	PF	PG	PH	PI	PJ	PK	PL
1967	QA	QB	QC	QD	QE	QF	QG	QH	QI	QJ	QK	QL
1968	RA	RB	RC	RD	RE	RF	RG	RH	RI	RJ	RK	RL

Fender Tube Chart Date Codes (Source: TDPRI.com)

Ampology 101

Leo Fender designed and began manufacturing instrument amplifiers in 1945. He strived to continuously make improvements in his circuits until his death in 1991. *Naked and Dimed* is only concerned with amps he made before 1968. These amps will be categorized as "tweed" (1947-1960), "brown," (1960-1963) and "black-face" (1964-1967). The tweed amps can be further subdivided into "TV-front," "wide-panel" and "narrow-panel." Only "narrow-panel" amps were used on *Naked and Dimed*. We'll use earlier tweed models on *Naked and Dimed II*.

Unlike audio amplifiers, which reproduce and enlarge input signals using components and circuitry that minimizes total harmonic distortion, the guitar amp is basically a low-fidelity signal processor. It's job is to allow an otherwise non-resonant plank of wood with steel strings to produce sound. The guitar *and* amplifier are essentially one instrument. That's why Fender guitars and amps made during the same period usually sound best together. They were made for each other.

Believe it or not, that signal coming out of your Telecaster is pretty bland. If you heard it enlarged perfectly through a high fidelity stereo amplifier, it would sound thin and wispy. However, if that signal is manhandled, squeezed, inverted, chopped, put back together and converted to mechanical energy by components that don't really care about distorting things a bit, it'll be fattened up considerably and sound pretty darn good.

Basically, the guitar's function is to influence how the amp's regulated DC power supply drives the output speakers. You strike a guitar string, the pickup under the string induces a small (less than a volt) alternating current signal, which enters your amplifier and causes a disturbance in the flow of electrons coming from the DC power supply circuit. That disturbance throttles the beam inside a vacuum tube as that beam zooms forward through the circuit, bringing along with it an enlarged version of the signal. This will happen twice, resulting in a much larger voltage signal in the output stage. That bigger signal is then transformed into mechanical energy so your ears can enjoy it. It's that simple.

The bottom line is that the signal caused by your vibrating guitar string is affected and colored by every component in the amplifier, including the ones that the signal doesn't even pass through. These include:

1. The DC power supply and rectifier,
2. The preamp and tone stack (especially tone stack location in circuit),
3. The phase inverter (for Class AB amps),
4. The power tubes,
5. The output transformer (OT),
6. The speaker(s),
7. The type of capacitors and resistors used in the circuit, and
8. The cabinet and baffle board.

I'll discuss which components matter most in each amp when addressing the individual models in the sections that follow.

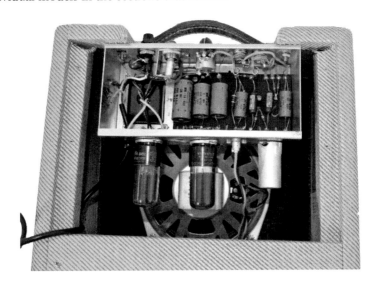

Higher Order Harmonics

I did everything I could to keep this book technically as simple as possible. However, there's one mathematical concept that must be mentioned. It will help us solve the riddle of why most of us prefer the simple, older tube amps over the later, better-designed ones. The fact is lo-fi tube amps produce higher order harmonics (i.e., distortion). It turns out that those higher-order harmonics are pleasing to the human ear. Leo Fender's strive for perfection tried to minimize that distortion. I guess some things were better left alone.

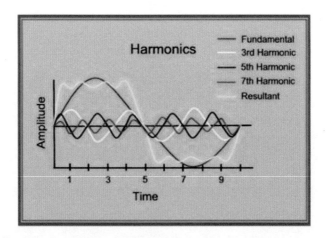

Odd Order Harmonics (Source: Quora.com)

The literature is mixed. Tom Wheeler says it's the "odd" order harmonics that make our old amps sound great. Dave Hunter says it's the "even" order harmonics. So is it even or odd? I asked for help explaining this phenomenon and Nic Grabien from the Tweed Amplifier Appreciation Society sent me the following write-up:

FROM NIC GRABIEN:

When a tube amp begins to distort, it's because the EVEN harmonics get out of balance from the levels they have, respectively, when the amp is running clean. The usual sinusoidal waveform of a musical note begins to "bulge," indicating that the 2nd harmonic is becoming relatively louder, compared to the root harmonic.

As the signal distortion increases, the 4th harmonic also becomes louder than normal, and the waveform gets lumpier. This is the "thickening" you hear in amps that are approaching breakup. In tweeds, this distortion happens because the power supply sags (small iron and low-value filter caps), to the root harmonic isn't amplified as much as the higher harmonics are. This is a part of the "sag and compression" we talk about and love so much in the tweeds.

However, once you actually hit the limit of what the power supply can do, the power stage clips. Now it's the ODD harmonics that get emphasized more than the evens, and the waveform flat-tops. This is when you start to get "crunch."

In Class AB push-pull amps that have cathode-biased output stages, this "crunch" has a different tonal makeup than what you get in fixed-bias Class ABs. In the fixed-bias Fenders, the harmonic content at clipping is different. The odd harmonics are usually stronger, making the crunch a smidge harsher. The trade-off is glassier highs when the amp is still in the "not quite clipping" stage, but you'll notice that the browns and blackface amps don't get that same sweet compression and sag. They don't "bloom" in quite the same way. (Also the later fixed-bias amps generally have bigger power supplies, which also keeps them from sagging. As a result, the "sweet spot" between clean and clipping is smaller, and is a tad harder to stay within if you're playing at that output level.)

So, if you're talking about bloom and thickness and sag and compression, it's even harmonics. If you're talking about crunch and drive and treble boost, it's odd harmonics.

It's why the High Power Twin is so distinctive: it does both very, very well. And, oddly enough, so does the original Harvard, which seems to have lucked into the perfect harmonic mix.

'65 Strat with '65 Vibrolux Reverb

My Black-Face Workhorses

Because I came of age in the late-70s, I had certain musical misconceptions. I already mentioned one of those was that I only played Fender and Gibson guitars. Another one was that I believed Fender black-face amps ruled supreme. I was pretty certain that if you had the black-face version of any Fender model, you had the best of the breed. Yes, rock n' roll elders talked about brown and tweed forefathers of the well-known models, but I didn't think it mattered all that much. Obviously, Leo Fender's final Pre-CBS designs were the pinnacle of his life's work and everything else done before that wasn't quite "there" yet. Thus, when I began my vintage amp exploration, I was pretty certain I'd confine my journey to only the black-face era. Besides, I already had three of the best known examples (the Super Reverb, Re-issue Twin Reverb and a Re-issue Deluxe Reverb).

'83 G&L with '64 Deluxe Reverb

1967 Super Reverb "The Beast"

Tube Chart

S/N	A 25441
Production	QH (1967-Aug), 56
Power/Output	117 volts, 40 watts
Speaker(s)	4 x 10 (Fender CTS)
PI	12AT7 Long Tailed
Rectifier	GZ34
Pre-amp	Normal: 7025 Vibrato: 7025, ½ 7025
Power Tubes	Fixed Bias (Adjustable) 6L6GCs
OT	Woodward Schumacher Interleaved 022855
Other:	Reverb Driver: 12AT7 Reverb Recovery: ½ 7025 Tremolo: 12AX7 (photoresistor)

Back in the old days when you saw someone standing in front of a Super Reverb, you knew they meant business. Most of my favorite guitar players in the Bay Area were lugging Super Reverbs and Vibrolux Reverbs in and out of their beat-up vans. That's why I bought "The Beast" when I saw it. I wanted to be a *bona fide* bluesman and knew having a black-faced icon like The Beast on stage behind me would be a vital prerequisite.

A 25441 was one of the last black-face Super Reverbs to leave the factory in the Fall of 1967. Serial number A 26000 would begin the silver-face era.

I don't remember exactly when I bought this Super Reverb, but it was in either 1988 or 1989. In those days I had a storage locker outside NAS Alameda. The Beast was kept there with all my worldly possessions until I got out of the navy. I wouldn't actually use it until I was a college student in 1990.

Here's what I *do* remember about buying this amp. It was sitting in the middle of Real Guitars. A group of guys stood around, marveling at it. The tag said $600. Someone behind the counter told everyone that the amp had once belonged to Robert Cray. Someone suggested that Stevie Ray might be interested (perhaps someone there had SRV's number on Rolodex). Everyone kept talking and no one was reaching for a wallet. I made my move. I tossed down six Benjamins and heaved The Beast away. Boy, that was a long haul back to Howard Street, where I had parked my car.

The Beast went to college with me after the navy. It would pretty much be my only amp for the next 18 years. My humble abode in San Luis Obispo had a mattress, K-Mart particleboard desk, Goodwill lamp, and this lofty and regal Super Reverb. The Beast was a vital piece of bedroom furniture back then. All my books and notebooks rested upon it. These things were tossed on the mattress when the amp was needed for a gig.

In those days I was the lead guitarist in the Low Rent Blues Band. Most of our shows were in dive bars or at house parties. Thus, there was never any sound guy. The singer just plugged a microphone into the normal channel of my amp.

I remember lamenting that I could only turn my Super Reverb volume up to 3. Nudging it any higher would cause people to stick their fingers in their ears and scream. I used a yellow Digitech PDS 1550 in those days and the "Classic Overdrive" B-channel gave me what I considered my signature tone.

I never dimed this amp when I was young. Hell, I probably never even turned it above 5. I was too afraid because I once saw a guy turn his Peavy 130 all the way up. It never got there. It whelped in pain, made a hissing sound, and died. I made a mental note never to do that with one of my amps.

Me and The Beast In My Office, 2003. I Stopped Cutting my Hair in 2003. Why Not? I Finally Got a Haircut in 2013 when my Kids Had Had Enough.

I mentioned earlier that I stopped using this amp when I became the lead singer for the P-Mooj. I would get shocked when any part of my body came in contact with the microphone. This Super Reverb was banished to a storeroom when the Re-issue Twin Reverb took its place.

Many years later I began exploring vintage Fender amps. Every book I read claimed the Super Reverb was one of the greatest blues amps of all time. I started thinking, "Hey, I have one!" I loved how my 1964 Deluxe Reverb sounded. I began to wonder how the old Super Reverb might compare. I decided to find out.

The Beast looked like Ben-Hur's mom and sister after they emerged from that Roman dungeon. I lugged him into a hallway and cleaned off all the dust and cobwebs. This old companion had been neglected for so long that I thought it might not power up, but it did. I grabbed a Telecaster, plugged it in, and began playing. "Nice." I turned the volume up a bit. "Even nicer." Then some more. "Really nice." Then a bit more. "Wow!" Then some more. "Wow!!!" I parked it on 10. "Holy crap!" My Super Reverb sounded incredible. No mush anywhere. Just crisp, tight, bold highs and lows. This was completely different than the Deluxe Reverb. Was it better? I wasn't sure. It was almost as if the Super Reverb was this rabid, raging beast and the Deluxe Reverb was Old Yeller.

I decided to put the The Beast back into service. I took him down to John Markovich in Tucson. The Super Reverb was finally safe to play again. John told me the original Holy Grail RCA 6L6GCs were extremely tired so he installed sparkling new Electro Hamonix 6L6s. The old RCAs came back to me in the new tube boxes.

The Beast sounded great when I cranked him up again. But, it wasn't exactly the same. Did it sound better or worse? I didn't know. I just knew I wasn't getting goosebumps like I did before. I reinserted the tired old RCA 6L6GCs and … *voilà*. That was it! It was then that I realized how crucial the tubes in a vintage amp were. I started buying and stockpiling NOS 6L6GCs and 6V6GTs. Hell, I even bought old 12AX7s and 7025s when I saw them. Vintage tubes are a must in vintage amps.

I'll probably never part with this Super Reverb (more for sentimental reasons than anything). Like I said, there *is* something wonderful about this amp. Few things excite me as much as standing in front of the 4 cranked CTS special design speakers when The Beast is roaring. True, there's hardly any touch sensitivity, but it certainly makes up for that when I attack an open E or A string.

The Beast Finally Gets to be on a Psychedelic Mooj Record!

The Super Reverb in a Nutshell ...

1. The dual 6L6GCs and 'big iron' interleaved output transformer (OT) gives this amp a firmness and low-end crispness like no other amp in my collection.

2. The tight bass response of the 4 x 10 CTS speakers make this amp hard to beat.

3. They don't refer to RCA 6L6GCs as the Holy Grail tubes for nothing.

4. Having a "Middle" tone knob is kind of cool, but it usually sits with the other tone knobs at 5.

5. In all the years I've played this amp, I've rarely use the bright switch. I've always preferred the "darker" sound of it being off.

6. My sloppy/choppy style was totally developed using this amp for 18 years. I'm convinced the GZ34 rectifier sag was a huge part of that sound.

7. I agree with everyone who says the Super Reverb is one of the greatest blues amps of all time.

8. Unfortunately, no sound guy is ever going to let you set the volume of this 40-watt monster anywhere near the point of breakup. You'll need an overdrive pedal for sure. You'll also give yourself a hernia lifting it up and over the edge of your car trunk. Then you'll have to heave it from the parking lot, around the venue, and in through the backdoor. Now do you remember why you gig with a Deluxe Reverb?

HEAR THE SUPER REVERB ON *NAKED AND DIMED*

When the album was almost finished I realized that I didn't use either the Deluxe Reverb or Super Reverb on anything. Yes, they had been brought to the studio (twice), but for some reason they were overlooked. Thus, I told Shane Matsumoto we needed one more song. We took an alternate take of "Sad Lonely People," stripped off all but the drums and bass and then I fired up the Super Reverb. I plugged in my 1969 Stratocaster and let it rip. What resulted became "A Super Reverb Deluxe Reverb Walk into A Bar."

I was horrified when I heard the playback for the first time. I seriously thought about just forgetting about the new song. Then I listened to the track again and realized that's how I played in my youth. It was as if I had gone back in time. I must have developed that choppy/sloppy style because I *was* using a Super Reverb. There's precision mixed in with all that chaos. All six strings are continuously clobbered but only one or two notes are allowed to ring out. Later in life, I'd become a bit more refined.

In the final mix Shane doesn't start the lead track until 1:07 so that you can only hear the '69 Strat and Super Reverb in the first 24 bars. I go out of my way to strike open E and A strings as often as I can. And how about that rectifier sag when I pause and attack?

"A Super Reverb Deluxe Reverb Walk into A Bar" might be considered filler to the *illuminati spotifidi* but I was happy to include it. If nothing else, it really gave me a good understanding of how different the Super Reverb and Deluxe Reverb really are.

1964 Deluxe Reverb

Tube Chart

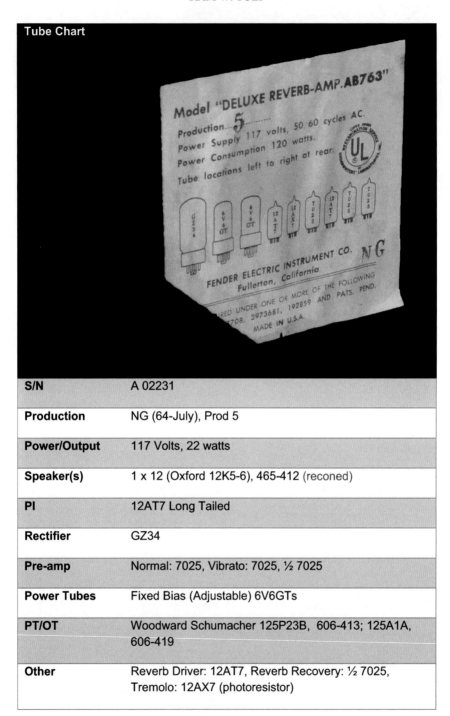

S/N	A 02231
Production	NG (64-July), Prod 5
Power/Output	117 Volts, 22 watts
Speaker(s)	1 x 12 (Oxford 12K5-6), 465-412 (reconed)
PI	12AT7 Long Tailed
Rectifier	GZ34
Pre-amp	Normal: 7025, Vibrato: 7025, ½ 7025
Power Tubes	Fixed Bias (Adjustable) 6V6GTs
PT/OT	Woodward Schumacher 125P23B, 606-413; 125A1A, 606-419
Other	Reverb Driver: 12AT7, Reverb Recovery: ½ 7025, Tremolo: 12AX7 (photoresistor)

Every vintage amp book I've read rants and raves about the Fender Deluxe Reverb. It's everybody's "desert island amp." By that they mean that if they were to be exiled somewhere for the rest of eternity and could only bring along one amp, it would be the Deluxe Reverb. No one ever asks these same people where they'd get the electricity.

I mentioned before that I used a '65 Deluxe Reverb Re-issue on stage for many years. It was an integral part of my *Analog Soup* and *Further than You Ever Knew* sound. My setup for those albums (and 100s of shows) was simply guitar (usually a '57 Vintage Re-issue Strat) into a Fulltone Clyde Wah, into a Fulltone OCD, into the amp (with the volume set as high as the soundman would allow ~3 or 4). The 1964 Deluxe Reverb replaced the re-issue Deluxe Reverb on stage in the summer of 2014.

This 1964 Deluxe Reverb was my only vintage amp for a long time. I had the Super Reverb, but like I said, it was sidelined due to its propensity to electrocute the innocent. Thus, I played this Deluxe Reverb—and only this Deluxe Reverb—for hours a day. I got to know it very well. The biggest difference between it and the re-issue was that the non-passive elements (mainly the power tubes) seemed to affect to a greater extent the overall flavor of the amp. I was getting this juicy, well-rounded, smooth, rich harmonic distortion from the fully-engaged 6V6GTs. It was a very comforting sound. The re-issue's tubes and overcrowded printed circuit board couldn't achieve anything like it.

This Deluxe Reverb is an early model, made in July, 1964. You'll notice it doesn't have the raised "Fender" logo on the grill or the numbers "1" and "2" above the inputs on both channels. They added that in 1965.

I truly love this amp. It's one I'll probably always use on stage even though other amps sound warmer and break up sooner. It's really because of that awesome reverb. I feel naked on stage without reverb.

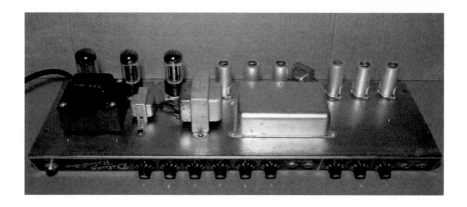

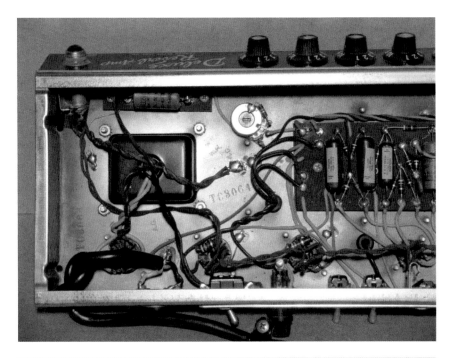

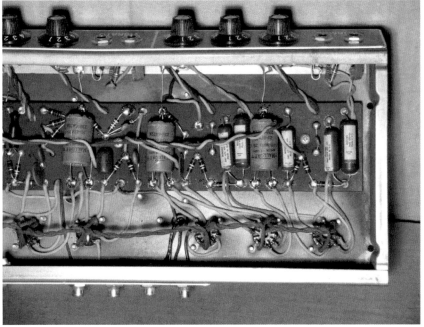

| The Deluxe Reverb in a Nutshell ... |

1. The 6V6GTs, undersized OT, and Oxford 12K5-6 gives this amp its signature sound.

2. This is one of the best sounding lead guitar amps you'll ever find.

3. This 22-watt wonder really is the perfect gigging amp. You can sometimes talk the sound guy into letting you crank it. If not, a transparent overdrive/boost will do wonders.

HEAR THE DELUXE REVERB ON *NAKED AND DIMED*

That's a G&L SC-2 and Les Paul R9 through the Deluxe Reverb doing the solos on "A Super Reverb Deluxe Reverb Walk into A Bar."

As I mentioned in the previous section, I had neglected to use the Deluxe Reverb on *Naked and Dimed*. I'd used a Deluxe Reverb (albeit a re-issue) on our previous albums and almost every recorded show we'd done so I figured no one would really miss it. If you knew the Psychedelic Mooj, you knew what a Deluxe Reverb sounded like. But since I was going through all the trouble of creating a new song for the Super Reverb, why not let the Deluxe Reverb tag along?

Beginning at 1:07 of "A Super Reverb Deluxe Reverb Walk into A Bar" you'll hear the G&L SC-2 begin soloing. The Deluxe Reverb volume is at 8 or 9. Then at 1:34 the R9 Les Paul takes over (volume turned down a notch). Then the SC-2 returns at 2:04. You get the picture. Odd solos are the G&L. Even numbered solos are the R9.

Do you hear the difference between the two amps? The smaller Deluxe Reverb is completely overdriven and the low-end gets mushy as soon I get aggressive. The Super Reverb holds down the fort no matter what's going on. These amps really are polar opposites of each other.

1964 Princeton Reverb

Tube Chart

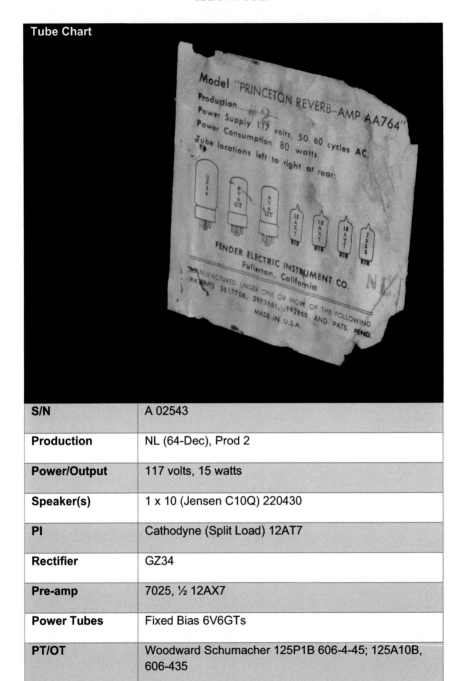

S/N	A 02543
Production	NL (64-Dec), Prod 2
Power/Output	117 volts, 15 watts
Speaker(s)	1 x 10 (Jensen C10Q) 220430
PI	Cathodyne (Split Load) 12AT7
Rectifier	GZ34
Pre-amp	7025, ½ 12AX7
Power Tubes	Fixed Bias 6V6GTs
PT/OT	Woodward Schumacher 125P1B 606-4-45; 125A10B, 606-435

By 2016 I had seven great amps in my collection. One thing was certain: the smaller the amp, the more I seemed to love it. Thus, I knew I needed to explore the Princeton Reverb. I was curious how it compared to the brown Princeton (my second favorite amp at the time) and the slightly larger Deluxe Reverb (my third favorite amp at the time). Turns out I would love it more than the Deluxe Reverb and almost as much as the brown Princeton.

I bought this Princeton Reverb from my good friend Tommie James. Several of my amps came from him. They were in his collection for decades. He loved them and cared for them like I loved and cared for my guitars. Although he had downsized his collection considerably before we met, he still had a few gems left and was willing to part with some when he learned about the *Naked and Dimed* album. In many ways, he was my mentor on the project and helped me organize the undertaking.

For weeks all I did was play the Princeton Reverb and the brown Princeton. These two low power marvels were side by side in the Mooj Cave. I'd plug into one and then the other (I'm not fancy enough to use a splitter). Although they were made only a year apart, they sound completely different. The Princeton Reverb has this sparkling, gritty snarl that is easily pushed into a crunchy overdrive. The brown Princeton is punchy and creamy. I love them both. Apologies to Dave Hunter for using his adjectives. But truthfully, no one describes how an amp sounds better than Dave.

Like the 1964 Deluxe Reverb I mentioned in the previous section, this 1964 Princeton Reverb doesn't have a raised logo on the grill. It does, however, have the numbers "1" and "2" over the single channel inputs.

FROM TOMMIE JAMES:

"This '64 Princeton Reverb was my go-amp in the studio after I purchased it from the original owner many years ago. It was a very nice original, one of the first Princeton Reverb's made in Dec., 1964 before Leo sold Fender to CBS. It has the original dust cover and footswitch and a great-sounding original-cone Jensen ceramic speaker. It was serviced by Clark Amps with the usual new caps, tubes, and grounded power cord. It got stored out of sight after a studio session in 2007, and when Bill asked if I owned one, I thought I had sold or traded it. Shortly afterwards, I came across it, called Bill, and he became the new owner in time to use it on the new album. I'm looking forward to hearing it again!"

The Princeton Reverb in a Nutshell …

1. This amp has the most "brown" feel of any of the black-face amps. That's because the tubes are driven at lower voltages and she's got a cathodyne (split-load) phase inverter.

2. The Jensen C10Q is a great little speaker. It's much darker than the Oxford 10J4 in my Princeton built just a year before.

3. I believe this was the last of the power tube grid bias tremolos. It sounds much better than the photocell throb in other black-face amps.

4. This is one of the best sounding lead guitar amps you'll ever find— even better than the Deluxe Reverb.

5. THIS would be my desert island amp!

HEAR THE PRINCETON REVERB ON *NAKED AND DIMED*

That's a '77 Tele through the Princeton Reverb playing fills and solos on "Dream Within a Dream." There's also a bit of 1963 Strat thrown in in the bridge section. Volume on amp for both guitars is maxed.

Initially, I used the 1963 Strat to do the solos. When I heard the final mix I realized they sounded just like the solos I had done on "Sad Lonely People." We were running out of time and money so I just let them be.

Then I realized that Christine (my beloved '77 Tele) wasn't used on the album. How could I be so cruel? To remedy this I scheduled one more session and brought Christine and the Princeton Reverb back to the studio. I told Shane I just wanted to overdub fills on "Dream Within a Dream." The original solos were removed and I added my Telecaster fills. Then we got creative and added harmony vocals instead of returning the Strat solos. Thus, a song that once had blazing guitar all over it became this calm, serene, dream-like thing (or should I say a dream-within-a-dream-like thing).

I saw an opportunity to add a bit of the Strat solo back in where there was a lull in the song (2:29 – 2:41). As you can hear, the Princeton Reverb sounds much brighter with the Strat.

Two of My Favorite Amps, Side by Side in the Mooj Cave.

Two Wonderful Amps, Doing What they Do Best.

1965 Vibrolux Reverb

Tube Chart	
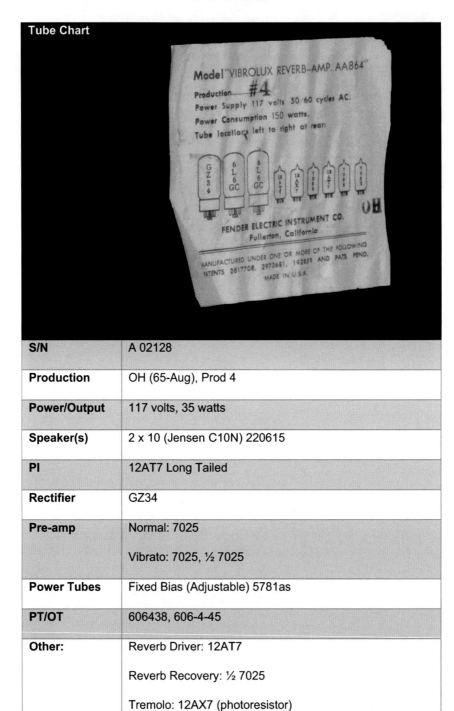	
S/N	A 02128
Production	OH (65-Aug), Prod 4
Power/Output	117 volts, 35 watts
Speaker(s)	2 x 10 (Jensen C10N) 220615
PI	12AT7 Long Tailed
Rectifier	GZ34
Pre-amp	Normal: 7025 Vibrato: 7025, ½ 7025
Power Tubes	Fixed Bias (Adjustable) 5781as
PT/OT	606438, 606-4-45
Other:	Reverb Driver: 12AT7 Reverb Recovery: ½ 7025 Tremolo: 12AX7 (photoresistor)

Tommie James told me many times that the Vibrolux Reverb was the best sounding black-face amp made by Fender. I didn't doubt Tommie; however, because I had a Super Reverb, Twin Reverb, Deluxe Reverb, and Princeton Reverb, I figured adding another black-face 6L6GC amp might be a bit underwhelming. How wrong I was.

Tommie sold me his favorite 1965 Vibrolux Reverb a few weeks before we began recording *Naked and Dimed*. He promised that I'd be blown away by it—and I was. In fact, I remember calling him from the studio to tell him so. This was the most-used amp on the album.

FROM TOMMIE JAMES:

Leo used 100% Allen-Bradley carbon-comp resistors that time proved to be an excellent choice. They hold their original values and are very dependable unless something else in the circuit goes wrong and causes them to fail.

After taking over in Feb. '65, CBS went with a lower-cost supplier, and this amp (made in Aug. '65) had about 60% A-Bs and 40% new-other from the factory. During the initial electronic restoration, Clark replaced all the cheap CBS resistors with new carbon-comp A-Bs.

The power tubes are Philips 5781as, rectifier is a Mullard, and pre-amp tubes are various USA brands. All were NOS and installed after I acquired the amp in 1999, and much experimentation was done using different tubes and speakers until I settled on the ones in it now. The hours on the tubes is unknown, but they are all still strong. This is the amp that I first used and fell in love with Philips 7581a power tubes.

The speakers are a matched pair of original-cone Jensen C10Ns made the 15th week of 1966. The original Fender-label Jensens are boxed and were sent to Bill. This is the amp that convinced me that there is a difference in "real" Jensen C10Ns and the Fender-labeled Jensens which don't sound as good. They also sound better to me than any Oxford 10 I've heard, and I have since accumulated a stash of nice original Jensen C10Ns.

The tone caps on the circuit board are Sprague Atoms installed in the original sleeves, and the filter caps under the cap can have been replaced twice since I've owned the amp. The ones in there now were new in about 2006 and have only a few hours on them.

The Vibrolux Reverb in a Nutshell …

1. There's some magic in that undersized OT.

2. Jensen C10Ns are the best sounding ceramic speakers ever made. I'm *sooo* tempted to put a pair in my 1963 Vibroverb.

3. It's because of this amp (and the 1963 Vibroverb) that I love the sound and feel of Fender 2x10 combos most of all.

4. Bottom line—this is the best sounding black-face amp in my collection!

HEAR THE VIBROLUX REVERB ON *NAKED AND DIMED*

You can hear the Vibrolux Reverb on "Last Goldtop Out of Kalamazoo," "Begging for Mercy," and "We All Know."

I brought the Vibrolux Reverb and Deluxe Reverb to the studio on the same day. I figured I'd use the Vibrolux Reverb with the 5-string Newman for the rhythm of "Last Gold Top Out of Kalamazoo" and then switch to the Deluxe Reverb and '82 goldtop for the slide solos and fills. However, the Vibrolux Reverb sounded so good that I just left it in place and switched guitars.

For some odd reason I also brought the Fender Electric XII that day. While the Vibrolux Reverb was still warm in the amp closet I plugged in the Electric XII and recorded the lead for "We All Know" on an alternate take of "I Know."

To add further insult to injury (to the Deluxe Reverb) I then did the solos for "Begging for Mercy" through the Vibrolux Reverb with my '68 Custom Telecaster.

I literally could not take the Vibrolux Reverb out of service that day. This was toward the end of the project and I was in a mindset of just getting things done. A damn good Deluxe Reverb almost get left off the album because of that.

Volume was set about 8 or 9. On "Begging for Mercy" I had the reverb turned the whole way up.

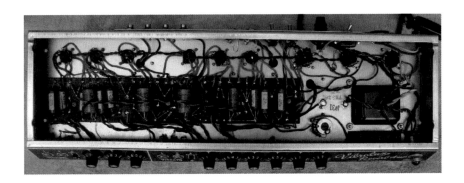

Last of the "FEIC" Front Plates.

Black-Face Reverb Amps Not Used on the Album

Although I have a Re-issue Twin Reverb in my collection, I didn't use it on *Naked and Dimed* because it's a re-issue. Even if I had an original Twin Reverb, I doubt I would have bothered lugging it into the studio. If we're being honest, the Twin Reverb isn't my kind of amp. I need something that can be pushed to distort. On our first two albums, the Twin Reverb Re-issue sounded great. But that was because its relentless headroom was defeated by an overdrive pedal.

Here's an aside (just because I'm thinking about it). Before I gave up the Mooj Cave, I took the Twin Reverb into the warehouse and dimed it. I just wanted once to hear it fully cranked. I got to 10 and it was still clean as a whistle—not even a hint of break up. Man, that thing was loud. It scared all the spiders and scorpions away.

When I made *Naked and Dimed* I didn't have my Pro Reverb yet. What a shame. 2x12 speakers and a tiny OT. Hello. It'll certainly be on *Naked and Dimed II*.

Let's also quickly mention the 1964 Vibroverb. I don't have one. Years ago, I talked with John Peden. I asked him what he thought about the black-face 1x15 Vibroverb. John told me that it would probably not be an amp I'd care much for (he was familiar with my playing style and the Psychedelic Mooj). He told me, "The black-face Vibroverb is a great jazz amp, but for rock n' roll and blues, find a Pro Reverb." Thus, to this day, I still don't have a 1964 Vibroverb. But I do have a Pro Reverb!

If I had to rebuild the black-face division of my amp collection from scratch, I'd probably bring back only a Vibrolux Reverb, Deluxe Reverb, and Princeton Reverb. Those amps give me everything I want and need. Did that sound too harsh? Okay. I'd also bring back a Pro Reverb.

A '66 Strat and '66 Pro Reverb. Both will be Featured on Naked and Dimed II.

Lo-Fi Rock n' Roll Machines

I mentioned John Peden in the previous section. I blame him for getting me hooked on Fender tweed amps. He sold me my 5E3 Deluxe. Once I met the 5E3, I felt the need to try every tweed amp Fender ever made. That journey isn't complete yet, but I'm making progress.

"Lily" Assembled this Fender Pro in May, 1956.

1956 Deluxe 5E3

Tube Chart

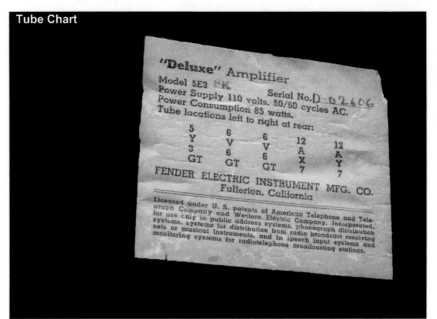

S/N	D-02606
Production	FK (56-Nov)
Power/Output	110 Volts, 15 watts
Speaker(s)	1 x 12 (Jensen P12R), 220951 (re-coned) 1959
PI	Cathodyne (Split Load) ½ 12AX7
Rectifier	5Y3GT
Pre-amp	12AY7, ½ 12AX7
Power Tubes	Cathode Biased 6V6GTs
OT	Triad and true

Exploring an old amp is like a religious experience for me. I take it very seriously and must prepare for it emotionally. The amp might arrive at noon, but I won't remove the packaging for hours. I'll just stare at the box. Then there's the unpack, unscrewing, and wire unravelling ritual. Then comes the gloved tube insertions, safety checks, and the handle integrity assessment. When I'm satisfied everything is in order, the plug is gently mated with a Brown Box dialed to 110 volts. Then the amp is switched on and the tube electrons slowly begin their thermionic emission mission. (For more about the Brown Box see https://www.amprx.net/.)

The day I played through this 5E3 for the first time I was simply stunned. I had never experienced amp nirvana like this before or again. I knew then and there I had entered a whole different world.

I use this amp a lot. I mean a lot. One thing I love about this amp is the interaction of the volume knobs. If you zero the unused channel volume, it really drives the amp. On *Naked and Dimed* I played around with the unused channel volume knob more than the actual channel volume knob. In the end, I just set it at the halfway point and fully clockwised the input volume. I thought about using a jumper cable to beef up the input but didn't. Oh, the wonderful places you can go with a 5E3.

This Immaculate 5E3 once Belonged to John Peden.

"Lupe" Put this Deluxe Together in November, 1956.

The Narrow-Panel Deluxe in a Nutshell ...

1. The push/pull circuit in this (and the other early Fender Class AB amps) produces some of the sweetest-sounding overdrive you'll ever hear. Scientifically, this is because the non-passive elements produce high (odd and even) order harmonics.

2. If ever there was a Lo-Fi amp, this is it. But somehow those Lo-Fi components make this amp one colorful signal processor.

3. The rectifier (5Y3GT) and tone stack location gives this amp incredible touch response. Later brown and black-face amps move the tone stack "left" toward the inputs in the circuit. The later amps trade a bit of that tweed magic for clarity and headroom.

4. I love the creamier, more compressed tones that result from using a cathodyne (split-load) phase inverter. This one seems to be the best at it.

5. Veteran guitar players have loved the crunch and warm, singing tube and/or speaker distortion produced by this amp for 65 years. Every overdrive pedal in the world is trying to duplicate this sound. Why not just have the real thing?

If I Could Have Used this 5E3 to do Leads on the Whole Album, I Would've.

HEAR THE DELUXE 5E3 ON *NAKED AND DIMED*

You can hear the Deluxe 5E3 on the lead track of "Who's Gonna Love Ya" and both rhythm and lead of "The Horseshit Song." The volume knob was fully clockwised for both songs. The unused channel volume was at 6.

I brought the '56 Deluxe to the studio twice. The first time was to use it with the '52 Telecaster to record the lead track for "Who's Going to Love Ya." We used the Bandmaster 5E7 and the '55 Esquire for the rhythm. You'd never be able to use the 5E3 on a "chunka-chunka-chunka" rhythm like we did with the 5E7. It would just have been mush.

The second time I brought the Deluxe 5E3 to the studio was to use it with the '55 Les Paul to record the rhythm track for "The Horseshit Song." I actually double tracked it. Then I plugged in the '52 Telecaster for the leads.

Here's the odd thing. In 1956 I could have used that very amp and those very same guitars to record something—but it would never have sounded like that. Once that volume knob began to distort the OT and Jensen speaker, my cowboy-booted compadres in the Buena Park Buckaroos would have told me to knock it off. Then the volume chickenhead would have had to be harmlessly set back to 3 or 4. Oh, the places you could have gone in 1956 ... but didn't dare (for ten more years).

1963 Champ 5F1

Tube Chart

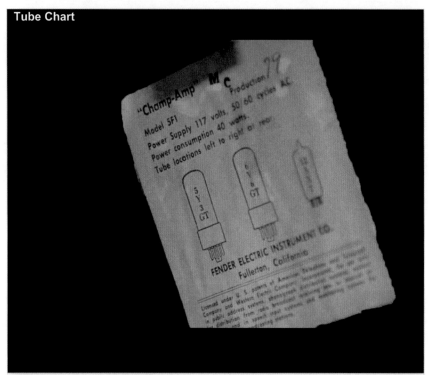

S/N	C 20209
Production	MC (63-Mar), Prod 79
Power/Output	117 volts, 4 watts
Speaker(s)	1 x 8 (CTS P8T)
PI	None
Rectifier	5Y3GT
Pre-amp	12AX7
Power Tube	Cathode Biased 6V6GT

This little Champ came into my life soon after the Deluxe. It was made in March of 1963. This would be near the end of the narrow-panel tweed Champs, made when all other models were wrapped in brown Tolex (and a few were even starting to leave the factory in black Tolex).

These narrow-panel Champs are relatively inexpensive and can be easily found in great shape. Everything on this 3-tube wonder is original. I almost feel guilty when I ravish her like I do. It's like putting drag racing miles on an original '66 Shelby Mustang GT-350. This amp loves it. She *wants* her lone chickenhead clockwised to the max.

Before recording *Naked and Dimed* I replaced all the original tubes. It sucked splitting up matched RCA 6V6GTs but my Martin 110 got the leftover and it was all good.

I can't say enough about this mighty little Champ. It actually spent more time in my office than the Mooj Cave because I liked to play when I was supposed to be working. It's the perfect bedroom amp but an ever better 'office door closed' amp.

The Narrow-Panel Champ in a Nutshell ...

1. As Dave Hunter would say, "One 12AX7 preamp tube, one 6V6 output tube, and a handful of capacitors and resistors (only a few of which the signal actually passes through), and there you are."

2. This model is only one of a few Class A amps made by Fender and it's a 4-watt monster.

3. Hands down, this was the most fun amp to use on *Naked and Dimed*. Shane Matsumoto never heard anything compress like this. He was surprised that such huge sounds came out of something so little.

Sounds Like a Stack of Marshalls!

HEAR THE CHAMP 5F1 ON *NAKED AND DIMED*

I used the Champ 5F1 for all solos on "Steal My Heart." Most of the solo is with the '55 Les Paul, but towards the end (starting at 5:07) the '55 Esquire is added. The LP is warm and smooth, like 30-year-old scotch. The Esquire is raw and gritty, like sock-poured hooch. The lone knob was, of course, set on 12.

The Champ was the champ. Hopefully, you'll be blown away with how great the '55 Les Paul sounds. I was. It sounded like I was playing in Royal Albert Hall through a stack of Marshalls.

Nothing Sounds Better than This!

1959 Bandmaster 5E7

Tube Chart

"Bandmaster" Amplifier

Model 5E7   Serial No. S03639

Power Supply 110 volts, 50/60 cycles AC.

Power Consumption 130 watts.

Tube locations left to right at rear:

5	6	6	12	12	12
U	L	L	A	A	A
4	6	6	X	X	Y
GA	GB	GB	7	7	7

FENDER ELECTRIC INSTRUMENT MFG. CO.

Fullerton, California

Licensed under U. S. patents of American Telephone and Telegraph Company and Western Electric Company, Incorporated, for use only in public address systems, phonograph distribution systems, systems for distribution from radio broadcast receiving sets or musical instruments, and in speech input systems and monitoring systems for radiotelephone broadcasting stations.

S/N	S03639
Production	IJ (59-Oct)
Power/Output	110 Volts, 26 watts
Speaker(s)	3 x 10 (Jensen P10R) 220937
PI	½ 12AX7 Cathodyne (Split Load)
Rectifier	5U4GA
Pre-amp	12AY7 (½ for each channel), 12AX7 and ½ 12AX7 (shared)
Power Tubes	Fixed Bias 6L6G or 5881
PT/OT	Uses same OT as 2x10 Super
Other:	Fender used a selenium rectifier in the bias circuit.

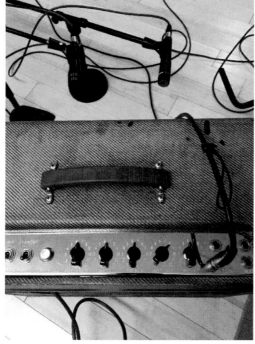

When one collects Fender amps, there are many surprises awaiting you. The best ones will come when you explore the "not quite 30-watt" 6L6 narrow-panel tweeds. Nothing in my collection sounds like this 1959 3x10 Bandmaster. Coming close are the '56 5E5-B Pro (will be discussed next) and my '55 5D8-A Twin (not used on *Naked and Dimed*).

People howl and profess about the glories of the 5E6-A Bassman. Yeah? Well, what if you had all that and it broke up at a much lower volume? *Then* you'd have the best sounding blues amp ever made!

A 5E6-A Bassman and 5D8-A Twin will be featured on *Naked and Dimed II*.

FROM TOMMIE JAMES:

The '59 3x10 Bandmaster is one of the best-sounding and most sought-after of Fender's narrow-panel tweed amps of the late 1950s. It's curious though that Fender had this 5E7 model in the lineup since it shared a chassis with the highly popular 2x10 5F4 Super, and 1x15 5E5 Pro which differed only in speaker compliment, output transformer, and occasional tweaks in chassis components. In fact, the 3x10 Bandmaster and 2x10 Super used the same 4-ohm transformer even though the 3x10's result in a 2.67-ohm load. Compared to the great-sounding 4x10 5F6-A Bassman, besides having one less speaker, the 3x10 Bandmaster is less powerful, lacks a "Middle" control, has an older style phase inverter, and less DC voltage to the output stage. The power output of this model was 26-30 watts vs. 40 for the Bassman. These technical differences result in a smaller sound and less overall volume with easier distortion when pushed. This amp has the original-cone Jensen P10Rs and the chassis components were 100% original when I saw it in a dealer ad and purchased it many years ago. It had been played a lot, and only the plug on the end of the power cord had been changed. Even the original caramel-colored dog-bone handle was still on the amp and in excellent condition.....very rare for a moderately-used '59 amp! Clark Amps installed new filter caps in the original Astron paper sleeves, NOS tubes, and a new grounded power cord were installed, and this is one great-sounding tweed Bandmaster! I've been a subscriber to *Vintage Guitar Magazine* for many years and Dave Hunter is one of my favorite writers because he often features interesting articles on vintage amps. I have enjoyed Dave's books on the technical details of vintage amps and communicated with him occasionally. He is always generous in answering my questions, and at some point I mentioned I had a '59 Bandmaster. Soon afterwards he asked if I would send photos and some comments for a possible article in *VG Magazine*. After many attempts at getting high-resolution photos of the views that satisfied the photo-editor, several pics were used in Dave's article about this amp on pages 44-47 in the Oct. 2016 edition. When Bill was selecting vintage amps for his new album, a 3x10 tweed Bandmaster was near the top of his wish-list, so this one is now in his collection and featured on the album where I can listen to it again and enjoy its wonderful sound forever.

The Narrow-Panel Bandmaster in a Nutshell …

1. The 3x10 5E7 Bandmaster, 2x10 5F4 Super, 1x15 5E5-A Pro, and 2x12 5E8-A "low-powered" Twin were essentially the same amp, other than speaker configuration and output transformers. These are my favorite amps made by Fender.

2. The Jensen P10R speakers used in this amp are regarded by many to be the best sounding speakers Jensen made.

3. Unlike the '59 Bassman (which this amp is often compared to), the Bandmaster has a smaller output transformer. It produces less power, yields a softer low-end response, and breaks up much quicker. Also, the Bandmaster uses a cathodyne (split-load) phase inverter.

4. You might have heard the term "parasitic capacitance" being bandied about by Fender amp lovers. It's used to describe an effect in Fender amps before the use of printed circuit boards. The wax-coated caps, cloth-covered wire, and carbon composite resistors soldered to terminal boards actually give off a unique 'background noise.' It almost sounds like a sort of reverb. I hear it with this amp and 5E5-B Pro more than the other tweeds.

An article about this very amp by Dave Hunter appeared in *VG* October 2016 issue:

https://www.vintageguitar.com/29075/fenders-5e7-bandmaster/

HEAR THE BANDMASTER 5E7 ON *NAKED AND DIMED*

Chavez played the '55 Les Paul through the 5E7 for the rhythm track of "Knocking on Your Door." Then I take the LP and play the T-Bone Walker section. You can hear how this amp responds differently to how Chavez and I play. Chavez plays very aggressively and I chug along gently, like I'm rowing a rowboat.

Chavez also used the '55 Esquire through the 5E7 for the rhythm of "Whose Gonna Love Ya."

1956 Fender Pro, 5E5-B

Tube Chart	
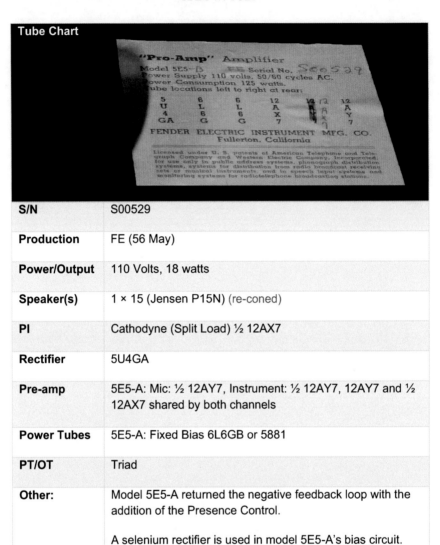	
S/N	S00529
Production	FE (56 May)
Power/Output	110 Volts, 18 watts
Speaker(s)	1 × 15 (Jensen P15N) (re-coned)
PI	Cathodyne (Split Load) ½ 12AX7
Rectifier	5U4GA
Pre-amp	5E5-A: Mic: ½ 12AY7, Instrument: ½ 12AY7, 12AY7 and ½ 12AX7 shared by both channels
Power Tubes	5E5-A: Fixed Bias 6L6GB or 5881
PT/OT	Triad
Other:	Model 5E5-A returned the negative feedback loop with the addition of the Presence Control. A selenium rectifier is used in model 5E5-A's bias circuit.

Tommie James was a great source of information in the early days when I was first trying to learn everything I could about Fender amps. One of the first conversations we had was about the 5E3 Deluxe. I told him I loved it but couldn't use it on stage or to jam with because the drums and bass would drown it out. He suggested I find a 5E5 Pro. It had the same circuit, but used 6L6s and had a 15-inch speaker. He assured me I'd love it.

I looked around and realized 5E5s were rare. I even considered settling for a 5D5 but they weren't around either. Tommie then suggested that I get in touch with his friend Michael Clark and have Michael build me a 5E5. I did; he did; and boy was I pleased with the result. This was actually a "one of a kind" build just for me. It wasn't the 5E5-A that he usually builds. It only has 3 knobs. It's really a 5E3 with 6L6s and 15-inch speaker. It's my "loud" Deluxe!

This Clark "5E5" was Built Just for Me! It's an Awesome Amp. I had Intended to Use it as a Stage Amp but the P-Mooj Stopped Doing Live Shows.

FROM TOMMIE JAMES:

Many years ago I got a call from a lady who said she heard I was interested in old musical equipment and asked me come over and look at a guitar and amp that belonged to her recently deceased husband. She opened a closet and invited me to pull out this 'heavy old amp and guitar.' The 'guitar' was a 1956 Fender 'lap steel' in the original case in mint condition. Then I removed the original dust cover from the amp and found a 1956 Fender Pro, also in near-mint (cosmetic) condition. The lady said her husband 'purchased them together in 1957 and used them a few times in a country/western band. Around 1960 he lost interest and stored them in that closet' .... where they remained untouched for the next 40 years! She said he refused to part with them, and they were too heavy for her to move after he passed away.

Without even turning on the amp or testing the guitar I bought both. I sold the lap steel (a beginner's model) and took the amp to Clark Amplification for evaluation and restoration.

Having been protected all of its life by the original dust cover, and kept in a closet out of the light, the original tweed still looks almost new. Everyone who has seen it person is stunned at the beautiful original cosmetic condition of the entire amp.

If everything works and it sounds good, an amp this nice should be left unaltered which usually protects and/or enhances the value, but electronically this one was unfortunately not playable. The filter caps had leaked badly and had to be replaced. The original Jensen 15" speaker still looked as-new, including the original paper cone as-viewed through the basket from the back of the speaker, so it was left alone.

When the amp was finally powered up for testing, on about the fourth guitar chord the original paper cone came apart at the surround from dry-rot, which couldn't be seen with the speaker still installed.

The original cone was beyond repair so the speaker was sent to Gregg Hopkins of Vintage-Amp Restoration in St. Louis with a request to re-cone it with parts as close as possible to the original.

It came back with a re-cone that looks identical to the original, and we finally got to hear the amp ..... and were not disappointed. It sounds as good as it looks!

> ### The Narrow-Panel Pro in a Nutshell ...
>
> 1. Similar in design to the Bandmaster, but has the 15-inch speaker. Now you got an amp that's as awesome as the Bandmaster but with a bigger speaker—that's a big deal!
> 2. If you only have one mid-size 6L6 narrow-panel tweed in your collection, it should be this one.

HEAR THE PRO 5E5-B ON *NAKED AND DIMED*

The '56 Pro came to the studio with my '55 Esquire. I used it to do the leads on "I Know." I play soft and gently and then speed up and play aggressively. The Pro keeps it together. It never falters. And, man, does it sound great.

I called Tommie James after I left the studio and told him how awesome the Pro sounded. He was delighted and said that it was probably the first time that old amp had been played like that since 1960.

Narrow-Panel Amps Not Used on the Album

I tried to "book-end" the narrow-panel era on *Naked and Dimed*. I used the Champ and Deluxe to highlight the low power 6V6 marvels and the Pro and Bandmaster to demonstrate the 6L6 higher watt wonders.

I didn't use the '55 Low Power Twin because I didn't have it yet. (That's why I have to make *Naked and Dimed II*.)

I still don't have a narrow-panel Super, but I'm looking!

I also didn't use the excessive force 40- and 80-watt tweeds that everyone rants and raves about. I plan to use a 1959 4x10 Bassman on *Naked and Dimed II*. Will I ever own a High Power Twin? I doubt it. I'd never be able to play it. The Psychedelic Mooj rarely plays big arenas. Hell, we don't even play dive bars anymore. Truthfully, I'm happy remaining in the 18-30 watt zone.

I have no excuse as to why I don't have a narrow-panel Vibrolux, Tremolux, Harvard, or Princeton.

If I had to rebuild the narrow-panel division of my amp collection from scratch, I'd bring them all back. I never met a tweed amp that I didn't like. In fact, I've loved every single one of them. Maybe I'll write a song about that someday.

'55 LP Twin with '58 Strat

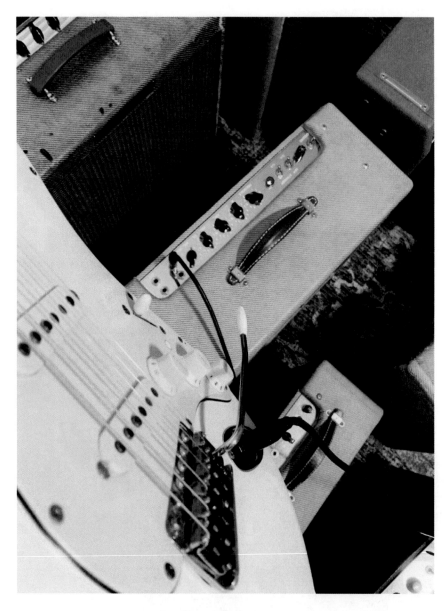

A '62 Strat Through the '56 Pro

The Wonderful Brown Amps

Do you wince when you hear someone professing the greatness of Fender brown amps? "Keep it quiet, bub," you whisper. "That's a secret we don't want getting out. You want them shooting up in price the way the tweeds did?"

If you're reading this book you're obviously a lover of Fender Fine Electric Instruments and know all about the brown amps. They lined the floors of music stores from 1960 to 1963. They came and went swiftly (like the wide-panel tweeds) because something better showed up within a few catalog cycles. Beginner and professional musicians alike eagerly upgraded. That's why it's so easy to find immaculate brown amps today. Most saw only a year or two of service and then got tucked away in closets while their black-face younger brothers endured 50+ years of continuous road abuse. Good thing there wasn't a war wood drive. These guys would have been chopped up for scrap.

Everything changed in 1960. These changes were profound. The cosmetic ones were obvious. The ones under the hood weren't visually noticeable but they certainly were aurally obvious. The creamy cathodyne phase inverters were phased out and stronger, more vibrant long-tailed inverters were ushered in. The non-student amps now had fixed bias power tubes. It was just a cleaner way to do things. The tone stacks were also moved "upstream" in the circuit, losing some of that cathode follower tweed touch sensitivity. These changes increased the output section's accuracy and power. Fender also started using feedback in most circuits. Many guitar players weren't sure what the Presence Knob did on the old big tweeds. Now they didn't even get to decide if they liked it or not.

To coincide with all this, one of the last vestiges of imperialism ended and the Belgium Congo became an independent nation. That meant the "Co" in "AlNiCo" wasn't cheap and abundant anymore. The "crisper" and "more resonant" Jensen Blue Bells were replaced on Fender factory shelves with cheaper, more durable ceramic-backed Oxfords. Changing speakers had a huge impact how the new Fender amps sounded compared to the old Tweeds.

Another change came with an upgrade in power and output transformers. Higher quality small layered and "big iron" interleaved OTs were now being supplied by Schumacher. The Triad guys were wondering why their phones weren't ringing anymore.

Yes, everything seemed to change in 1960. I guess the biggest change was Fender went from a little company making lots of amps to a big company making even more amps. And what great amps they were.

1963 Princeton 6G2

Tube Chart

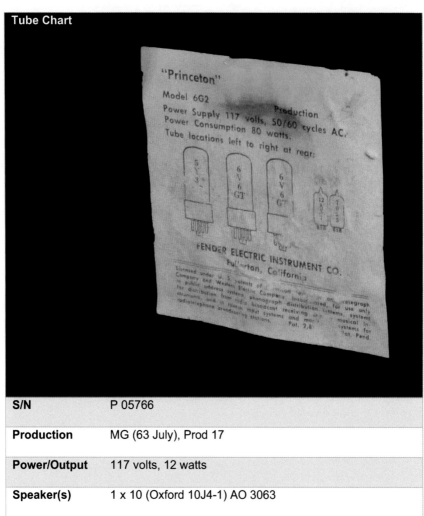

S/N	P 05766
Production	MG (63 July), Prod 17
Power/Output	117 volts, 12 watts
Speaker(s)	1 x 10 (Oxford 10J4-1) AO 3063 Weber Ferromax 10F150 / 127 90417 currently installed.
PI	Cathodyne (Split Load) half of 12AX7
Rectifier	5Y3GT
Pre-amp	12AX7 and 7025
Power Tubes	Fixed Bias 6V6GTs
PT/OT	Woodward Schumacher 125P1A 606-307, 125A10B 606-315

Here I was, totally in love with my narrow-panel Deluxe and it's simply wasn't loud enough to use when I wanted to use her most. What if there was an amp that had a similar feel *and* a bit more power? There was! It was the 6G2 Princeton.

The Princeton 6G2 used on *Naked and Dimed* (P 05766) was made in July, 1963. I have her original Oxford 10J4-1 speaker (AO 306312) but it had been replaced by the previous owner with a Weber Ferromax 10F150 and I never switched it back. This was the only amp used on *Naked and Dimed* that didn't use a period correct speaker.

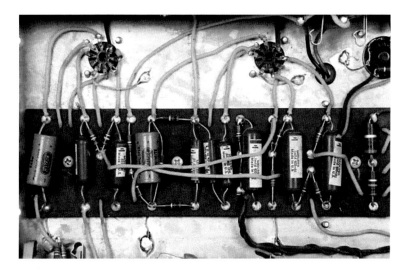

I actually have a mint 1962 6G2 "museum piece" Princeton (P 04024) but didn't use it on the album because it arrived just as I was about to record the 6G2 tracks. I decided to use P 05766 instead of P 04024 because P 05766 had been my go-to gal for years. I didn't want to "cheat on her."

The Princeton 6G2 is one of my favorite amps of all time. You know how Neil Young has a barn full of narrow-panel Deluxes? If I were famous, I'd be the guy with a barn full of brown Princetons.

Now, I wouldn't say it's as good as the Deluxe but it certainly comes darn close. And it's definitely louder. Its greatest asset might be that it's almost as good as the Deluxe but costs 60% less. Whenever I talk to people who are truly tone conscious and just getting interested in buying vintage amps, I tell them to start here.

This was my first Fender brown amp. Needless to say, after meeting the 6G2, I would go on a brown amp buying binge. Everyone talks about the reverb-soaked black-face models and the majestic tweeds. Nary a mention is made about these transitional JFK-era gems. Good. That'll make them easier to find for the true amp aficionados out there.

This is the Oxford in my '62 Princeton

The Brown Princeton in a Nutshell ...

1. The fixed-bias 6V6s give this amp some loudness and sparkling clarity, but the OT and cathodyne (split-load) PI keeps it sounding and feeling like a narrow-panel Deluxe.

2. The 5Y3 rectifier and lower plate voltages give this amp great touch sensitivity.

3. The simple volume-modulating tremolo on the 6G2 Princeton is nothing like the harmonic vibrato you'll find on the big brown amps. It adds to the tactile feel of this amp—you play hard, it's gone; you ease up, it returns. I love it.

4. Maybe the lone 10-inch speaker is a bit underwhelming at times. They actually make a brown Princeton Re-issue with a 12-inch speaker now. I haven't tied it but I bet it sounds awesome.

HEAR THE PRINCETON 6G2 ON *NAKED AND DIMED*

I recorded the solos for "Knocking on My Door" using this amp at full volume with the '57 hardtail Strat. If you listen closely, you'll hear that terrific brown Princeton tremolo. It cuts out when I attack and creeps back in when things calm down a bit.

While the 6G2 was still warm I plugged in the 1963 Strat and a 1963 Reverb Unit and did the solos on "Sad Lonely People." Just listen to that soaking wet reverb. Does your onboard black-face reverb sound like that? Hell no.

If you're lazy and use an overdrive pedal, you can get a nice warm harmonic distortion from any amp with little or no effort. If you're a tone purist like me and want your amp to do all the work, you gotta play the hell out of that guitar. I never worked so hard in my life driving that little brown Princeton on "Sad Lonely People." I literally tore the strings off (well, the E string anyway).

1961 Deluxe 6G3-A

Tube Chart	
	"Deluxe" Amplifier
	Model 6G3 4 Production 59
	Power Supply 117 volts, 50/60 cycles AC. Power Consumption 70 watts min., 110 w. max. Tube locations left to right at rear:
	G 6 6 12 12 7
	Z V V A A 0
	3 6 6 X X 2
	4 GT GT 7 7 5
	FENDER ELECTRIC INSTRUMENT MFG. CO. Fullerton, California
	Licensed under U. S. patents of American Telephone and Telegraph Company and Western Electric Company, Incorporated, for use only in public address systems, phonograph distribution systems, systems for distribution from radio broadcast receiving sets or musical instruments, and in speech input systems and monitoring systems for radiotelephone broadcasting stations. Pat. 2,817,708 & Pat. Pend.

S/N	D 00668
Production	KJ (61 October), Prod 59
Power/Output	117 Volts, 20 watts
Speaker(s)	1 x 12 (Jensen P12R), 220022 (1960)
PI	Long-Tailed 12AX7
Rectifier	GZ34
Pre-amp	Normal: ½ 7025, Bright: ½ 7025, ½ 12AX7 (common to both channels)
Power Tubes	Fixed Bias 6V6GTs
PT/OT	Woodward Schumacher 606117, 606121
Other	Tremolo: ½ 12AX7 (Bias Vary)

I loved the brown Princeton so much that I had to explore something that was supposedly just like it but a bit louder. I wasn't disappointed. This 6G3 (D 00668) was built in October, 1961 (Production 59) and came equipped with the last of the highly-desired Jensen P12Rs (220022).

This amp has the creamiest overdrive you'll ever hear. The guy who sold it to me said that the "harmonic saturation and punctuated presence is highly unique." Boy, was he right. During Mooj Cave jams, I'd often switch between this amp and the brown Princeton and really couldn't tell much of a difference. Moojmates Dave and Rick, however, both thought the Princeton sounded better than this Deluxe. I kind of agree now that I've listened to the *Naked and Dimed* tracks. The brown Deluxe does, however, sound better than the black-face Deluxe Reverb. Maybe better isn't the right word. It sounds more rock n' roll-ish.

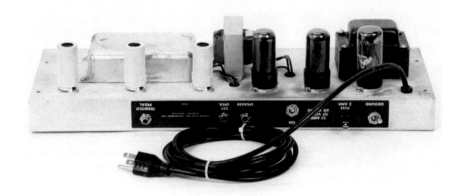

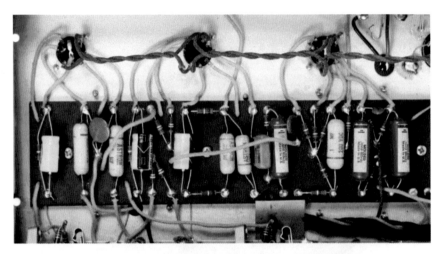

This amp was utilized for many of the rhythm tracks on *Naked and Dimed.* I'm not sure why I didn't do at least one solo with it. It's definitely a better lead guitar amp than a rhythm guitar amp.

The Brown Deluxe in a Nutshell ...

1. All the vintage amp literature will tell you that the 6G3 isn't as warm and crunchy as the 5E3 but certainly not as bright and rigid as the Deluxe Reverb. True. But you really have to hear the 6G3 for yourself. It's got a nasty, raunchy, raw sound that cannot be adequately described in a book.

2. This, my friends, is the sound of rock n' roll!

HEAR THE DELUXE 6G3 ON *NAKED AND DIMED*

We paired the brown Deluxe with the '57 hardtail Strat. It was used on "You Know" and the rhythm track of "Begging for Mercy." Volume was set at 8 and the tone knobs were at 5. For "Begging for Mercy" I have the vibrato maxed out.

It was also used with the '69 Strat to play the rhythm track for "Sad Lonely People." We originally did the track using the '69 Strat through the '60 Bandmaster. That sounded awful. We almost cheated and used a Klon Centaur to get it to break up a bit but didn't. I had the brown Deluxe at the studio and so Chavez redid the track through the Deluxe. It sounded better (at least the amp distorted). Now that a year has passed and I listen to the song I realized the '69 Strat is still too harsh through the brown Deluxe. This is a good example of why grey bottom pickups don't really sound best in brown or tweed amps.

1963 Vibroverb 6G16

Tube Chart

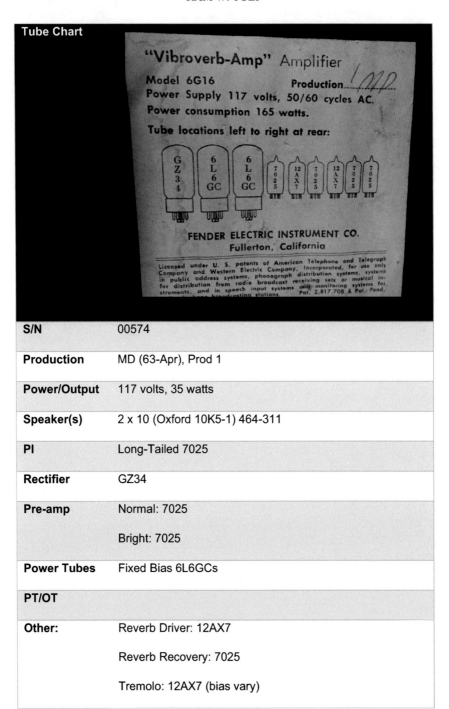

"Vibroverb-Amp" Amplifier
Model 6G16   Production
Power Supply 117 volts, 50/60 cycles AC.
Power consumption 165 watts.

Tube locations left to right at rear:

FENDER ELECTRIC INSTRUMENT CO.
Fullerton, California

Licensed under U. S. patents of American Telephone and Telegraph Company and Western Electric Company, Incorporated, for use only in public address systems, phonograph distribution systems, systems for distribution from radio broadcast receiving sets or musical instruments, and in speech input systems and monitoring systems for broadcasting stations. Pat. 2,817,708 & Pat. Pend.

S/N	00574
Production	MD (63-Apr), Prod 1
Power/Output	117 volts, 35 watts
Speaker(s)	2 x 10 (Oxford 10K5-1) 464-311
PI	Long-Tailed 7025
Rectifier	GZ34
Pre-amp	Normal: 7025 Bright: 7025
Power Tubes	Fixed Bias 6L6GCs
PT/OT	
Other:	Reverb Driver: 12AX7 Reverb Recovery: 7025 Tremolo: 12AX7 (bias vary)

By the end of 2014, I had six incredible amps (Super Reverb, Deluxe Reverb, narrow-panel Deluxe, narrow-panel Champ, brown Princeton and brown Deluxe). I probably could have stopped there but I knew I needed to do a bit more exploring. Next, I delved into the Fender brown 6L6 amps.

There's this legend going around that the 1963 brown Vibroverb is as rare as hen's teeth. I remember thinking I'd never find one. Today, every time I turn around I see one for sale, and it's usually going for less than what the price guide says it's worth. True, most don't have their original Oxford speakers ... but, don't many folks yank them out anyway?

Before we had met, Tommie James had downsized his collection considerably. But he still had some great amps. In 2015 he sent me an article in *Vintage Guitar Magazine* written by Dave Hunter, entitled "25 Most Valuable Amplifiers." We discussed the article on the telephone. Then Tommie said, "I still have #5 and #10." My eyes darted to the list and I saw that #5 was the 1959 Bandmaster and #10 was the 1963 Vibroverb. I'm not sure how I did it, but I somehow talked Tommie out of his beloved Vibroverb. (A year later I bought the Bandmaster, too.)

Is all the hype about this amp true? I think so. I love this amp. It's got a great full, thick tone. When she's pushed, she distorts nicely. The 6L6CGs make it more versatile than the smaller 6V6 browns. By that I mean you can use it for rhythm guitar and it's nice to actually hear the better-defined bass.

The Brown Vibroverb in a Nutshell ...

1. The brown Vibroverb uses the same OT as the Vibrolux Reverb, which is why both 2x10 amps sound so incredible.

2. This was Fender's first amp with on-board reverb.

3. To accommodate tremolo and reverb in the same circuit, the tremolo from the tweed-era Tremolux amp was used. This smooth, volume-modulating pulse is loved by many.

FROM TOMMIE JAMES:

The Vibroverb is a very rare Fender amp. Only 500 serial numbers were assigned to this unique chassis, and only a handful have ever been seen for sale. This was Fender's first amp with on-board reverb, and in order to put tremolo and reverb in the same circuit, the tremolo from the tweed-era Tremolux amp was used. There was no way they could fit the great brownface-era tremolo (that used 2.5 tubes to operate it) plus reverb controls into a reasonably-sized combo amp cabinet with 2 x 10s. So, the Vibroverb was a short-lived experiment in early 1963 that became one of the best 2 x 10 combo amps Fender ever made. I got this one in a trade many years ago, and it was (and still is) in pristine cosmetic condition. The circuit had been worked on previously by someone who had replaced a dozen or so resistors and installed new filter caps. Michael Clark returned it to 100% original Allen-Bradley carbon-comp resistors, re-capped it, installed NOS tubes, and it sounds amazing! It has the original Oxford ceramic speakers with rare brown plastic magnet covers with "Fender" molded into the plastic. These are seen only in early to mid-1963 Fender combo amps. It was apparently too complicated (and costly) to keep the Vibroverb circuit in the product line, so in 1964 it became the new black-face Vibrolux Reverb model with the new pulsating photo-cell vibrato technology. The Vibrolux Reverb circuit used the same transformers as the Vibroverb that produced about 40 watts of power. This was another amp I never intended to part with, but I was hooked on the opportunity to hear it again on Bill's album project and let it go to another good home.

HEAR THE VIBROVERB 6G16 ON *NAKED AND DIMED*

We used the 1963 Stratocaster through the 1963 Vibroverb on several rhythm tracks. Chavez is cranking her on "I Know" and "We All Know." I actually removed lots of the fills and solos in the first half of "I Know" so you could totally focus on the Strat and Vibroverb. We also used it for the rhythm track on "Steal My Heart." The OT and two Oxfords completely saturate when we push things. And the 6L6GCs really hold the low end together. No other brown amp sounds like that.

These Oxfords Distort Like No Other Speaker. They Give The Vibroverb its Very Unique Tone.

'61 ES-350T with '63 Vibroverb

1960 Bandmaster 5G7

Tube Chart	

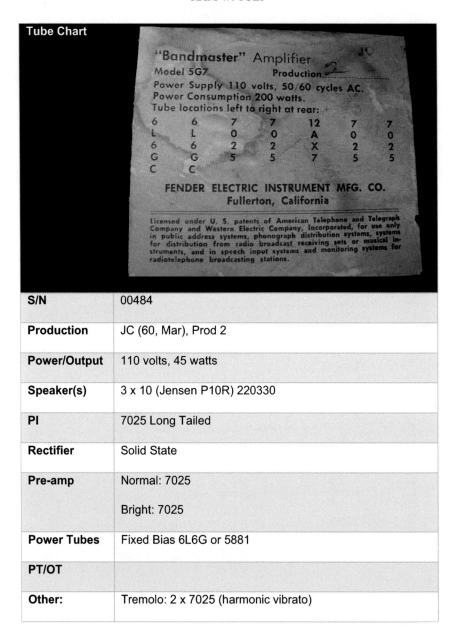

"Bandmaster" Amplifier
Model 5G7   Production 2
Power Supply 110 volts, 50/60 cycles AC.
Power Consumption 200 watts.
Tube locations left to right at rear:

6	6	7	7	12	7	7
L	L	0	0	A	0	0
6	6	2	2	X	2	2
G	G	5	5	7	5	5
C	C					

FENDER ELECTRIC INSTRUMENT MFG. CO.
Fullerton, California

Licensed under U. S. patents of American Telephone and Telegraph Company and Western Electric Company, Incorporated, for use only in public address systems, phonograph distribution systems, systems for distribution from radio broadcast receiving sets or musical instruments, and in speech input systems and monitoring systems for radiotelephone broadcasting stations.

S/N	00484
Production	JC (60, Mar), Prod 2
Power/Output	110 volts, 45 watts
Speaker(s)	3 x 10 (Jensen P10R) 220330
PI	7025 Long Tailed
Rectifier	Solid State
Pre-amp	Normal: 7025 Bright: 7025
Power Tubes	Fixed Bias 6L6G or 5881
PT/OT	
Other:	Tremolo: 2 x 7025 (harmonic vibrato)

What a difference 5 months makes. My narrow-panel Bandmaster was shipped in October, 1959 and this "brownish-pink" one was shipped in March, 1960. If any two amps showcase how many changes were made transitioning from the "sit in back of" to the "stand in front of" amps, it's these two guys. Just about everything changed.

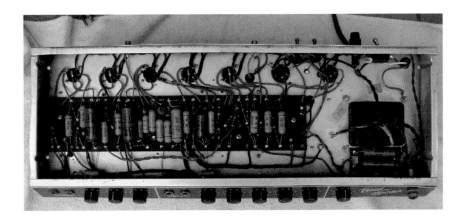

The Brown Bandmaster in a Nutshell ...

1. Considered by Paul Linden to be cleaner sounding than any of the tweeds but dirtiest-sounding out of the large browns.

2. Like all the brown Professional Series amps, this Bandmaster has the legendary harmonic vibrato.

An article about this very amp by Dave Hunter appeared in VG April 2017 issue:

https://www.vintageguitar.com/31881/fenders-1960-bandmaster/

FROM TOMMIE JAMES:

'60 3x10 Bandmaster This very rare March 1960 model 5G7 amp has the unique features of the very first brown Fender amps, such as the rough pink-brown Tolex, tweed-era grill cloth, light-brown faceplate with matching color in the flat logo tail, center-mounted Volume controls, RCA speaker plug, and mysterious Pulse-Adjust (on the rear faceplate) with a plugged hole. The new front-mounted controls are in the order "Bass, Treble, Volume" (same order as on the tweed amps), and are commonly referred-to as early "Center-Volume" amps. By May '60 this had been changed to the more common "Volume, Treble, Bass", and the circuit is a very different amp from the 5E7 tweed Bandmaster. It has the same 4-ohm output transformer and 3 P10R Jensens, but has a long-tailed-pair phase inverter, and the 67233 power transformer puts out about 500-515 DC volts compared to the tweed's 400-410. It has a larger bass response making them cleaner with later break-up than the tweeds. Its tone is generally cleaner than the tweed but dirtier than the other brown Tolex 40-watt models. The additional power routinely blew the P10R Jensens, as was the case with this amp which went back to the factory in 1963 for repairs that included 3 new P10R's that have somehow survived. Like the other new Fender Professional Series amps in 1960, this amp also has the first version of the new vibrato circuit with the original single-button footswitch. I got this amp in a trade many years ago, and the only circuit change was a later output transformer. It was serviced by Clark Amps with new caps in the original Astron paper sleeves, a new custom-wound 2.67-ohm output transformer, an adjustable bias pot was added, and a grounded power cord and NOS tubes were installed. It is now a great-sounding example of this ultra-rare model, and it was featured in a follow-up article on Fender's 3x10 Bandmaster amps by Dave Hunter in the April 2017 edition of Vintage Guitar Magazine on pages 36-39. Bill added it to his collection in time to use it on the new album!

HEAR THE BANDMASTER 5G7 ON *NAKED AND DIMED*

Chavez played the '55 Les Paul through the brown Bandmaster for the rhythm track of "Dream within a Dream." We tried the '69 Strat first and it sounded horrible (bright and brittle). The Les Paul was the only guitar that could get it to break up nicely.

Relentless Headroom

1961 Concert 6G12-A

Tube Chart	

"Concert-Amp" Amplifier

Model 6G12   Production ___ KB

Power Supply 110 volts, 50/60 cycles AC.
Power consumption 200 watts.

Tube locations left to right at rear:

5	5	7	7	12	12	7	7
8	8	0	0	A	A	0	0
8	8	2	2	X	X	2	2
1	1	5	5	7	7	5	5

FENDER ELECTRIC INSTRUMENT MFG. CO.
Fullerton, California

Licensed under U. S. patents of American Telephones and Telegraph Company and Western Electric Company, Incorporated, for use only in public address systems, phonograph distribution systems, systems for distribution from radio broadcast receiving sets or musical instruments, and in speech input systems and monitoring systems for radiotelephone broadcasting stations.

PAT. 2,817,708 & "PAT. PEND."

S/N	02947
Production	KB (61 Feb), Prod 21
Power/Output	110 volts, 40 watts
Speaker(s)	4 x 10 (Jensen P10PF) 220116
PI	7025 Long Tailed
Rectifier	Solid State
Pre-amp	Normal: 7025 Bright: 7025
Power Tubes	Fixed Bias 5881s
PT/OT	45249, 606048
Other:	Tremolo: 2 x 7025 and ½ 12AX7 (6G12-A) (harmonic vibrato)

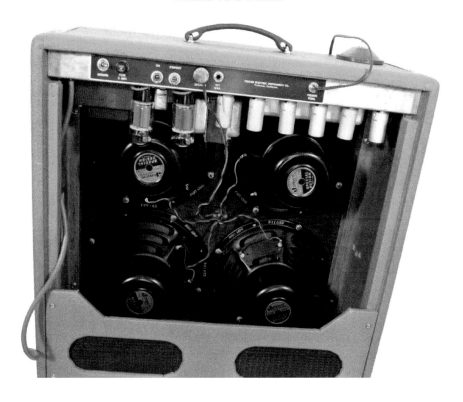

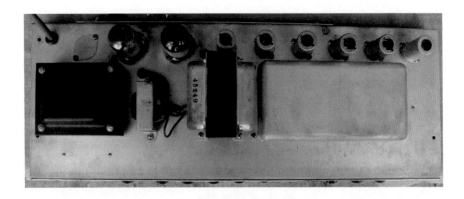

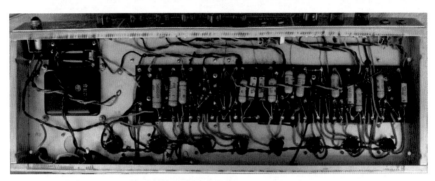

As I was getting ready to start *Naked and Dimed* I wondered if I was overlooking anything. I called Tommie James and asked him what his favorite amp was. He didn't even hesitate. "The brown Concert," he said. I didn't have one because I was averse to big amps. In fact, by this time in my collecting days I was ignoring the 40 watt amps. But was I missing out by not even considering a brown Concert?

Tommie had a few left in his collection and he sold me the one he thought sounded best. Yep, it was love at first hear.

'61 SG Special with '61 Concert

FROM TOMMIE JAMES:

This Concert has the original maroon (aka Oxblood) grill cloth, original Tolex. The brown Tolex is final version (rough-brown), and the circuit has the final-version vibrato that the brown-face Fender amps are famous for.

This is the 6G12-A. The letter "A" was supposed to be hand-written on the tube chart, but often the "A" was omitted by the person at Fender who was responsible for installing the correct chart. This chart is missing the "A."

The speakers have been upgraded from the original (tired) P10Qs to Jensen P10PF (alnicos) that have heavier "N" size magnets and have been re-coned by Weber speakers with 1.5" (N) voice coils, 3" vented center dust caps, and premium ribbed guitar cones. New magnet covers are installed with new Jensen silver-blue labels that are identical to the originals seen on Jensens beginning in the late 1950s.

This amp has not been used enough for the speakers to be broken in. They sound great as-is, but will sound even better with some more hours of playing time.

Original Power & Output trannys are the same as in the '60 5F6-A tweed Bassman. Electronic restoration was done in 2006. Filter caps have 2006 date codes and are like new. Power tubes shown are NOS Philips 7581As and re-biased.

Bias board has new SSR diodes & bias pot has been added. Circuit was in transition from yellow Astrons to blue Mallorys, and original Astron pre-amp caps are upgraded to new Sprague Atoms.

All original (Allen-Bradley) resisters and molded caps were checked, and replaced as needed.

HEAR THE CONCERT 6G12-A ON *NAKED AND DIMED*

I knew I wasn't going to get that Concert to overdrive no matter what I did so I knew no guitar leads were going be done with it. But what about laying down some bass lines? And why not use the Dano UB-2? Wow. What resulted was something completely out of this world: "Knox County Line." Shane stopped me from adding anything on top of just the drums and bass. He told me to leave the studio because he had an idea. He said it would be easier to show me than try to explain it. I went off, hung out with the front desk guys for a bit, then came back. Shane recorded all those overlapped vocals. "What'da think?" he asked. I loved it!!!

The harmonic vibrato is a mind-melter. No crappy photocell killjoy there!

The Brown Concert in a Nutshell ...

1. Not going to Lie. You won't be playing any down-home blues on this thing.
2. A very "sweet sounding" amp. Listen to the Ventures first album and you'll know what I mean by that.

Brown Amps Not Used on the Album

Just like the narrow-panel tweeds, I wanted to "book-end" the browns. I used the Princeton and Deluxe to highlight the low power side and the Bandmaster and Concert to demonstrate the "Professional Series" high power end. The Vibroverb is also a great representative of the "in between" browns.

I'm probably done adding to my brown amps. There are still many that I don't have. These include the Pro, Super, Vibrosonic, and Vibrolux. I also don't have the blonde Twin. Nor do I have any of the piggy backs. For now, I'd rather just look for the missing tweeds. However, because I'm a huge Mark Knopfler fan, I will keep my eyes open for that elusive brown Vibrolux.

1967 Ampeg B-18-N Portaflex

I got this Ampeg bass rig from Tommie James in 2016. It's actually a restored 1967 B18N head on a new B15 cabinet with a JBL D140F speaker. A B18N head has twice the power of a B15N (60 vs. 30 watts), and the D140F handles it with ease and has great bass tone.

FROM TOMMIE JAMES:

I got the idea for this amp from Ampeg inventor Jess Oliver after he had restored one of his Oliver P502A, a B15N, and a B18N amp for me between 2004-06. We became friends during this time, and I learned a great deal from him about those amp models.

I was intrigued that the B18N had twice the power of the B15N. Jess told me that after the B18N was introduced in late 1963, the "Latin guys" from NYC discovered that a B18N head would fit into the same tray that held the B15N head and began special-ordering a B18N head on a B15 cabinet with the optional JBL D130 speakers available at the time. They would out-perform all the other bass amps being used in NYC clubs and other venues at the time…same Ampeg B15N tone with twice the power!

In 2008 I located and got Jess to restore a nice original '64 B18N head and had his friend (and now one of mine) Mark Gandenberger in Cincinnati custom-build a B15N cabinet to the exact specs of Jess's original double-baffle design, and cover it in Blue-Check Tolex exactly like Ampeg used on the original cabinets in the mid-1960's. I installed a nice original-cone JBL D140F which had not been available during the mid-1960's, and the resulting sound was awesome!

As of Sept. 2019, I have duplicated this 6 more times using B18N heads from 1964-67, and cabinets made by Mark in Cincinnati who now has a company called Vintage-Blue. They sold quickly when I listed them for sale. Jess Oliver passed away in June 2011, and my Ampeg head electronic restorations are being done by Steve Hunter in Athens, GA who has learned how to get the heads to sound better than when new.

When Bill was looking for a bass amp to use on his new album I was completing restoration of this 1967 B18N head on a new Vintage-Blue B15 cabinet w/original-cone JBL D140F. He became the new owner and liked it so much no other bass amp was used to record all the songs on the N&D album !!

HEAR THE AMPEG B-18-N ON *NAKED AND DIMED*

The Ampeg was used on every song except "Knox County Line." We used the 1963 P-Bass for all tracks except "The Horseshit Song." For that one I used the UB-2. The B-18 volume was set at 5 for the whole session. Only once did I crank it up to 10 and that was for "Begging for Mercy."

An Egregious Oversight was that this 1990 Jazz Bass Plus was Left Off the Album. It was Given to Me by My Girlfriend/Future Wife for Christmas, 1990. You May Have Spotted it in My College Room Picture on Page 41.

DISCOVER THE PSYCHEDELIC MOOJ!

https://g.co/kgs/xWLKDF

https://www.youtube.com/user/psychedelicmooj

Naked and Dimed

"Who's Gonna Love Ya?" - Rick Obenshain: Drums; Richard Chavez: Rhythm Guitar ('55 Esquire through '59 Bandmaster); Bill Tuli: Bass ('63 P-Bass through '67 B-18-N), Lead Guitar ('52 Telecaster through '56 Deluxe), and Vocals.

"Dream Within a Dream" - Rick Obenshain: Drums; Richard Chavez: Bass ('63 P-Bass through '67 B-18-N) and Rhythm Guitar ('55 Les Paul through '60 Bandmaster); Bill Tuli: Lead Guitar ('77 Telecaster and '63 Stratocaster through '64 Princeton Reverb) and Vocals; Shane Matsumoto: Backing Vocals.

"Knox County Line" - Rick Obenshain: Drums; Bill Tuli: 6-String Bass ('58 Danelectro/Spiegel UB-2 through '61 Concert); Shane Matsumoto: Vocals.

"I Know" - Rick Obenshain: Drums; Richard Chavez: Bass ('63 P-Bass through '67 B-18-N) and Rhythm Guitar ('63 Stratocaster through '63 Vibroverb); Bill Tuli: Lead Guitar ('55 Esquire through '56 Pro) and Vocals.

"A Super Reverb and Deluxe Reverb Walk into a Bar" - Rick Obenshain: Drums; Bill Tuli: Bass ('63 P-Bass through '67 B-18-N), Rhythm Guitar ('69 Stratocaster through '67 Super Reverb), and Lead Guitar ('83 G&L SC-2 and '07 Les Paul R9 through '64 Deluxe Reverb).

"Knocking on Your Door" - Rick Obenshain: Drums; Richard Chavez: Rhythm Guitar ('55 Les Paul through '59 Bandmaster); Bill Tuli: Bass ('63 P-Bass through '67 B-18-N), Lead Guitar ('57 Stratocaster through '63 Princeton), and Vocals.

"You Know" - Rick Obenshain: Drums; Richard Chavez: Bass ('63 P-Bass through '67 B-18-N) and Guitar ('57 Stratocaster through '61 Deluxe); Shane Matsumoto: Vocals.

"Begging for Mercy" - Rick Obenshain: Drums; Richard Chavez: Rhythm Guitar ('57 Stratocaster through '61 Deluxe); Bill Tuli: Bass ('63 P-Bass through '67 B-18-N) and Lead Guitar ('68 Telecaster Custom through '65 Vibrolux Reverb); Christina Lanza: Vocals.

"Horseshit Song" - Rick Obenshain: Drums; Bill Tuli: 6-String Bass ('58 Danelectro/Spiegel UB-2 through '67 B-18-N), Rhythm Guitar ('55 Les Paul through '56 Deluxe), Lead Guitar ('52 Telecaster through '56 Deluxe), and Vocals; Shane Matsumoto: Backing Vocals.

"Sad Lonely People" - Rick Obenshain: Drums; Richard Chavez: Bass ('63 P-Bass through '67 B-18-N) and Rhythm Guitar ('69 Stratocaster through '61 Deluxe); Bill Tuli: Lead Guitar ('63 Stratocaster through '63 Reverb Unit and '63 Princeton) and Vocals; Christina Lanza: Backing Vocals.

"We All Know" - Rick Obenshain: Drums; Richard Chavez: Rhythm Guitar ('63 Stratocaster through '63 Vibroverb); Bill Tuli: Bass ('63 P-Bass through '67 B-18-N) and 12-String Guitar ('66 Electric XII).

"Steal My Heart" - Rick Obenshain: Drums; Richard Chavez: Bass ('63 P-Bass through '67 B-18-N) and Rhythm Guitar ('63 Stratocaster through '63 Vibroverb); Bill Tuli: Lead Guitar ('55 Les Paul and '55 Esquire through '63 Champ) and Vocals; Shane Matsumoto: Backing Vocals.

"Last Goldtop out of Kalamazoo" - Rick Obenshain: Drums; Richard Chavez: Bass ('63 P-Bass through '67 B-18-N); Bill Tuli: 5-String Guitar ('15 Newman through '65 Vibrolux Reverb) and Slide Guitar ('82 30th Anniversary Les Paul through '65 Vibrolux Reverb).

I've Read Every Book Written about Guitars and Amps

ANALYSIS OF VINTAGE FENDER AMPLIFIER VALUES

How much do vintage Fender amps cost these days? The highest priced ones according to the *2019 Vintage Guitar Price Guide* are shown in Table 1.

Table 1. The Most Expensive Fender Amps (2019)

Amp	Current Value
Narrow-Panel HP Twin (2x12)	$19,000
Narrow-Panel LP Twin (2x12)	$13,500
Narrow-Panel Bandmaster (3x10)	$9,500
Narrow-Panel Bassman (4x10)	$9,500
Wide-Panel Twin (2x12)	$8,700
Blonde Twin (2x12)	$8,500
Brown Vibroverb (2x10)	$8,100
Narrow-Panel Super (2x10)	$7,800
V-Front Super (2x10)	$6,500
V-Front Dual Professional (2x10)	$6,000
Narrow-Panel Deluxe (1x12)	$5,700
Wide-Panel Super (2x10)	$5,100
Black-Face Vibroverb (1x15)	$5,100
Blonde Dual Showman (Piggy Back)	$4,900
Narrow-Panel Pro (1x15)	$4,900
Brown Bandmaster (3x10)	$4,500
Blonde Showman 12 (Piggy Back)	$4,500
Wide-Panel Bandmaster (1x15)	$4,400
Blonde Showman 15 (Piggy Back)	$4,200
Narrow-Panel Tremolux (1x12)	$4,100
Wide-Panel Pro (1x15)	$4,000
Narrow-Panel Vibrolux (1x10)	$4,000
Blonde Bassman (Piggy Back)	$3,900

If you wanted to collect Fender amps, would that be a financially wise thing to do? Unless you started this collection twenty years ago, probably not. Therefore, your motives now must be purely to find joy and pleasure in a hobby that enriches you in a way that losing a bit of money won't matter. What follows in this section is an analysis of vintage Fender amplifier values since 2001. The data comes from *Vintage Guitar Magazine Price Guides*.

Since I try to buy only immaculate amps (they must be cosmetically perfect), this data reflects high-end values. "Road-relic'd" amps typically sell for 25 - 30% less. If the amp has been recovered, has replacement speakers, or doesn't have the original "iron," i.e., transformers, then the amp should be bargain-priced at about half the high-end value.

The vast majority of my amps are museum pieces. It's hoped that one day they will go to a museum. But for now they're played—and I do mean played. Thus, they must be maintained in perfect working order. All have three-prong plugs and non-leaking electrolytic filter caps. Some also have—gasp—re-coned speakers. Truthfully, what good is an all original amp if it sounds screechy, scratchy, flappy, and dull? You've defeated the whole purpose of why you're even playing a vintage amplifier.

These days the "rule of 35" is very much in effect. According to Nate Westgor, amps over 35 lbs. or 35 watts—like Super Reverbs and Concerts— aren't desired much anymore. They languish on the selling sites and usually don't move unless the seller drops the price once or twice. Small, low-power amps—like the Princetons and Deluxes—sell quickly. They'll also go for more than the price guide says they're worth. Next year, that little combo amp you're ogling might be 10% more. Better grab it now if you can.

Figure 1 shows the value of vintage Fender amps from 2001 to 2019. The value of most more than doubled in that period. Some standouts soared. Today, for example, the narrow-panel High Power Twin is worth an amazing $19,000, almost 4½ times what it was worth in 2001 (See Figure 2).

The data in Figure 1 will be broken out separately in the sections that follow so I won't clutter it with a legend (but if you're impatient, jump ahead to Figure 7 to see which amps really mattered). Table 1 can also be used to identify the amps soaring above the others.

An important observation in Figure 1 is that there wasn't a significant "bubble" for amplifiers like there was for vintage guitars. The High Power Twin might have lost 17% of its value in 2010, but it quickly rebounded within a few years. Vintage guitars *never* regained their pre-bubble momentum (see Figure 4).

Amp values didn't "crash" in large part because they weren't being scooped up by speculators, hoping to cash in on the pre-2008 vintage instrument craze. Everyone knows guitars get all the glory and amps get little or no respect. Thus, people buying vintage amps were and still are typically "tone conscious players," collecting something they want to use, not hang on the wall behind a glass case.

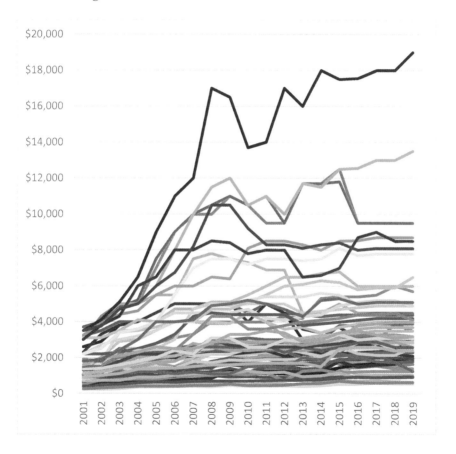

Figure 1. Vintage Fender Amp Values Since 2001

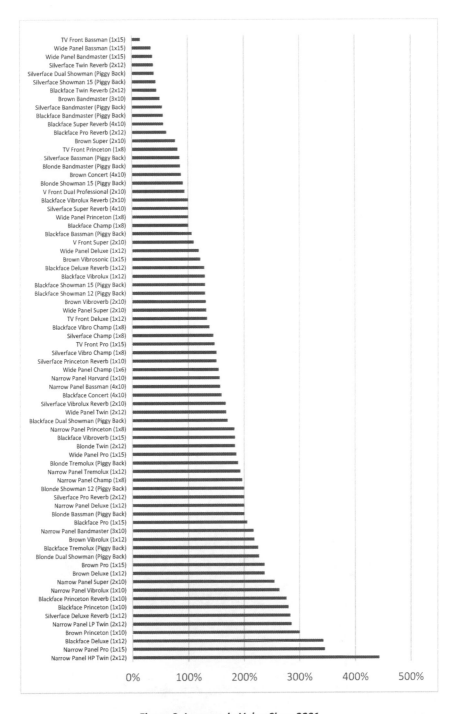

Figure 2. Increase in Value Since 2001

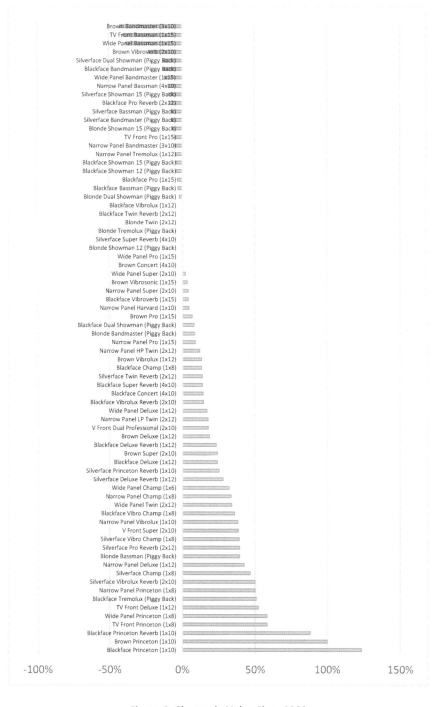

Figure 3. Change in Value Since 2009

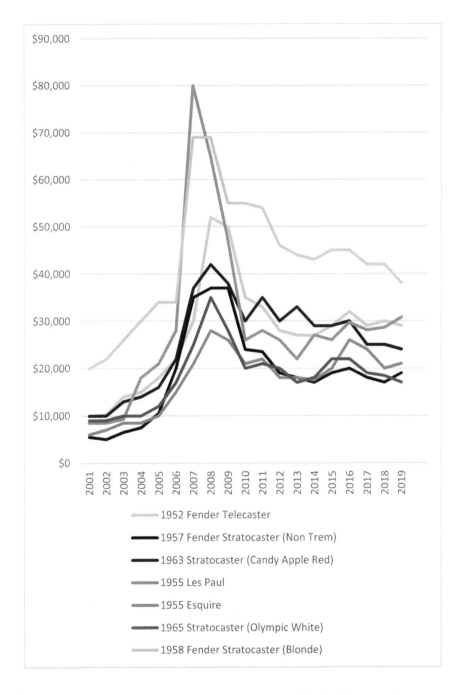

Figure 4. Values of the Rarest Guitars in my Collection Since 2001

By comparing the 20-year and 10-year trends (see Figures 2 and 3), you can see the vintage amp market has really shifted in recent years. Small amps are where it's at these days. I saw it in my own life. Twenty years ago, I gigged with a Super Reverb. Now, I gig with a Deluxe Reverb. It's about tone *and* saving my 56-year-old back. But it's also about something else: the magic found in a low-powered amp. Hey, that's what this book was all about!

Table 2. Amps with Greatest Appreciation Since 2001

Amp	20-y
Narrow-Panel HP Twin (2x12)	443%
Narrow-Panel Pro (1x15)	345%
Black-Face Deluxe (1x12)	343%
Brown Princeton (1x10)	300%
Narrow-Panel LP Twin (2x12)	286%
Silver-Face Deluxe Reverb (1x12)	283%
Black-Face Princeton (1x10)	280%
Black-Face Princeton Reverb (1x10)	276%
Narrow-Panel Vibrolux (1x10)	264%
Narrow-Panel Super (2x10)	255%
Brown Deluxe (1x12)	237%
Brown Pro (1x15)	237%
Blonde Dual Showman (Piggy Back)	227%
Black-Face Tremolux (Piggy Back)	225%
Brown Vibrolux (1x12)	218%
Narrow-Panel Bandmaster (3x10)	217%
Black-Face Pro (1x15)	205%
Blonde Bassman (Piggy Back)	200%
Narrow-Panel Deluxe (1x12)	200%
Silver-Face Pro Reverb (2x12)	200%
Blonde Showman 12 (Piggy Back)	200%

Table 3. The Only Amps with Meaningful Appreciation Since 2009

Amp	10-y
Black-Face Princeton (1x10)	**124%**
Brown Princeton (1x10)	**100%**
Black-Face Princeton Reverb (1x10)	88%
TV-Front Princeton (1x8)	58%
Wide-Panel Princeton (1x8)	58%
TV-Front Deluxe (1x12)	52%
Black-Face Tremolux (Piggy Back)	51%
Narrow-Panel Princeton (1x8)	50%
Silver-Face Vibrolux Reverb (2x10)	50%
Silver-Face Champ (1x8)	47%
Narrow-Panel Deluxe (1x12)	43%
Blonde Bassman (Piggy Back)	39%
Silver-Face Pro Reverb (2x12)	39%
Silver-Face Vibro Champ (1x8)	39%
V-Front Super (2x10)	38%
Narrow-Panel Vibrolux (1x10)	38%
Black-Face Vibro Champ (1x8)	36%
Wide-Panel Twin (2x12)	34%
Narrow-Panel Champ (1x8)	33%
Wide-Panel Champ (1x6)	32%
Silver-Face Deluxe Reverb (1x12)	28%
Silver-Face Princeton Reverb (1x10)	25%
Black-Face Deluxe (1x12)	24%
Brown Super (2x10)	24%
Black-Face Deluxe Reverb (1x12)	23%

Table 4. Amps with Lowest Appreciation Since 2001

Amp	20-y
TV-Front Bassman (1x15)	15%
Wide-Panel Bassman (1x15)	35%
Wide-Panel Bandmaster (1x15)	38%
Silver-Face Twin Reverb (2x12)	39%
Silver-Face Dual Showman (Piggy Back)	40%
Silver-Face Showman 15 (Piggy Back)	43%
Black-Face Twin Reverb (2x12)	44%
Brown Bandmaster (3x10)	50%
Silver-Face Bandmaster (Piggy Back)	54%
Black-Face Bandmaster (Piggy Back)	56%
Black-Face Super Reverb (4x10)	56%
Black-Face Pro Reverb (2x12)	62%
Brown Super (2x10)	77%
TV-Front Princeton (1x8)	81%
Silver-Face Bassman (Piggy Back)	85%
Blonde Bandmaster (Piggy Back)	86%
Brown Concert (4x10)	88%
Blonde Showman 15 (Piggy Back)	91%
V-Front Dual Professional (2x10)	94%

Table 5. Amps with Greatest Depreciation Since 2009

Amp	10-y
Brown Bandmaster (3x10)	-42%
TV-Front Bassman (1x15)	-40%
Wide-Panel Bassman (1x15)	-38%
Brown Vibroverb (2x10)	-23%
Black-Face Bandmaster (Piggy Back)	-13%
Silver-Face Dual Showman (Piggy Back)	-13%
Wide-Panel Bandmaster (1x15)	-12%
Narrow-Panel Bassman (4x10)	-10%
Silver-Face Showman 15 (Piggy Back)	-9%
Black-Face Pro Reverb (2x12)	-9%
Silver-Face Bandmaster (Piggy Back)	-8%
Silver-Face Bassman (Piggy Back)	-8%
Blonde Showman 15 (Piggy Back)	-7%
TV-Front Pro (1x15)	-5%
Narrow-Panel Bandmaster (3x10)	-5%
Narrow-Panel Tremolux (1x12)	-5%
Black-Face Showman 12 (Piggy Back)	-4%
Black-Face Showman 15 (Piggy Back)	-4%
Black-Face Pro (1x15)	-3%
Black-Face Bassman (Piggy Back)	-3%
Blonde Dual Showman (Piggy Back)	-2%

The Tweed Amps

There are three distinct eras for Fender tweed amps: TV-front, wide-panel and narrow-panel. Each will be studied separately.

TV-Front Tweeds (1947 – 1952)

TV-front Fender amps have always been popular. They were the amps that put Fullerton, California on the map. Suave and good-looking guitar players could finally sit up front next to the crooners and yodelers. Nothing being sold at the time could match Fender amps for volume, bass response, *and* sound quality. Bob Crooks and the Standel boys up in South San Gabriel may have given Leo a run for his money in the early years, but that didn't last long. Leo Fender will forever be known as the guy who killed the big band era and made guitar-dominated small combo bands possible. He may not have liked rock n' roll, but he'll go down in history as its patron saint.

The most valuable models from this era don't even have TV-fronts (see Figure 5). They're the V-Front Dual Professional and V-Front Super. These *style-paquebot* heptagons come up for sale every now and then and I've been tempted to buy one. They go for a bit more than a really good narrow-panel Deluxe these days. Maybe one day Billy Gibbons will part with his enormous V-Front collection and there'll be a glut in the market. It'll be like the great tulip crash of 1637, but for Truman-era amplifiers.

The TV-front Deluxe and Pro will always be amps that cowboys throw their hats up into the air and hoot and holler about. No one has ever complained about them. In fact, most people rant and rave about their legendary grime and grit. I have a 1951 Deluxe that I love. Give me that lo-fi paraphase inverter and cathode biased circuit any day. I didn't use my 5A3 on *Naked and Dimed* because it wasn't in my collection when the album was recorded. But you can bet your bucket of beer it'll be on *Naked and Dimed II*. For now, let's hope the original speaker holds out I don't need to replace any of the metal envelope 6SN7 tubes. Can you even find them? I have no idea.

These days the TV-front Princeton seems to be gaining the most traction. No surprise there. Any Fender amp with "Princeton" in the name will find an eager buyer.

The only model that seems to be a dud is the 1x15 Bassman. Play a bass through it and you'll blow the speaker. Well, that's what we've been told all these years. Sadly, when someone calls a vintage dealer and tells them, "I got an old Bassman in the barn," the dealer will frown after he drives 100 miles, jogs across the pasture, and sees this one under a bale of hay in the barn. It's currently down 40-percent from its 2011 high.

Table 6 shows how the values of TV-front models have changed over time. Most of the growth was before the bubble of 2008. Since 2008, there have only been modest gains and some have even lost value. Rather than repeat that statement over and over again, I'll mention here that every table that follows will show a similar trend for the larger amps (over 22 watts). The small, low powered amps climb modestly through the years and then take off about 2014.

I should probably also point out that the 20-y column isn't quite 20 years yet. It's as of 2001 so I guess that would be 18 years. I have data that goes all the way back to 1991 but didn't include that in this analysis because the vintage market exploded in 2002. Between 1991 and 1999 amps had a relative annual rate of appreciation of about 15%. In 1999 amps dipped a bit but regained their footing and then shared to a lesser extent in the post 2002 vintage guitar frenzy (compare Figures 1 and 4).

Table 6. TV-Front Amp Change in Value

Amp	10-y	20-y
TV-Front Bassman (1x15)	-40%	15%
TV-Front Deluxe (1x12)	52%	**133%**
V-Front Dual Professional (2x10)	18%	94%
TV-Front Princeton (1x8)	58%	81%
TV-Front Pro (1x15)	-5%	**147%**
V-Front Super (2x10)	38%	**110%**

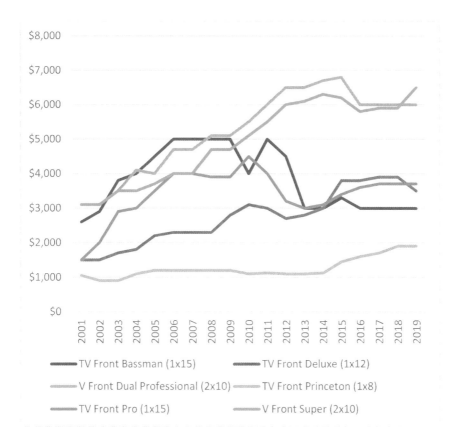

Figure 5. TV-Front Models

Wide-Panel Tweeds (1953 – 1954)

The wide-panel tweeds came and went so quickly that you hardly see them around much these days. They used to track nicely with the other tweeds but now hold steady at their 2010 values (see Figure 6). Suffice it to say, they'll never be as popular as the narrow-panel amps that came right afterwards.

Again, it's all about the little amps. If you're in it for the riches, seek out the Champ, Princeton, and Deluxe. Luckily, they'll also be the ones that sound best, too.

Actually, the wide-panel Twin is still somewhat popular. It's a damn good amp. They come up for sale every once in a while but if they're priced too high, they'll just sit. People like them but not enough to pay more than they would for a narrow panel Bandmaster or Bassman.

Truthfully, I've always been somewhat leery of the wide-panel era after reading Ritchie Fliegler's *Amps! The Other Half of Rock 'N' Roll*. He, Mitch Colby, and John Peden played a Les Paul, Stratocaster, and Telecaster through every iteration of the Pro Amp. Their ears concluded that the wide-panel Pro was kind of a dud compared to the previous TV-front and latter narrow-panel versions. I'm probably wrongfully assuming that that would be the case for the Deluxe too. (I've been told by many to play through the wide-panel Deluxe before I make such an egregious across-the-board declaration. So I will. Chances are I'll have one in my collection by the time we do *Naked and Dimed II*.)

Here's an aside since we're name dropping here. A few years ago I told Harvey Moltz about the *Naked and Dimed* project. He said, "I have to introduce you to my friend Ritchie Fliegler!" I was so excited. Ritchie Fliegler is my amp hero. I was all set to write down Ritchie's number but somehow left without getting it. Later, I saw Ritchie comment on something on Facebook. I messaged him and asked if it would be okay to call him. He was probably reluctant but agreed. I began the conversation with, "Harvey Moltz wants to introduce us and ..." I forget what Ritchie said after that but it was pretty funny. It was something along the lines of, "Since Harvey never mentioned you to me I can only guess that he wasn't being serious." Ritchie was actually very nice. I told him what I was doing but he had no interest in it. He did, however, wish me good luck.

Table 7. Wide-Panel Amp Change in Value

Amp	10-y	20-y
Wide-Panel Bandmaster (1x15)	-12%	38%
Wide-Panel Bassman (1x15)	-38%	35%
Wide-Panel Champ (1x6)	32%	**154%**
Wide-Panel Deluxe (1x12)	17%	**119%**
Wide-Panel Princeton (1x8)	58%	**100%**
Wide-Panel Pro (1x15)	0%	**186%**
Wide-Panel Super (2x10)	2%	**132%**
Wide-Panel Twin (2x12)	34%	**168%**

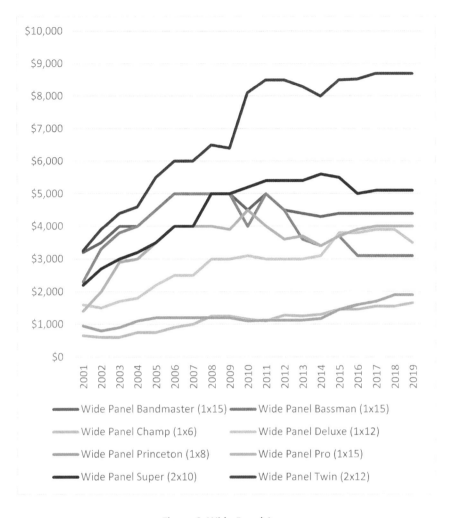

Figure 6. Wide-Panel Amps

Narrow-Panel Tweeds (1955 – 1960)

This is where all the growth has taken place in the vintage amp market for the past 20 years (see Figure 7). *These* are without a doubt the most desirable amps ever made by Fender. In 2001, you could have bought an excellent condition example of every narrow-panel amp for $23,825. Today, that collection would be worth a whopping $84,700 (that's a 256% increase). That's better than the NASDAQ in the same period by over a factor of 2!

I should point out that there are slight variances in narrow-panel tweed values because early models differ a bit from the latter models. An example would be 4-inputs vs. 2-inputs for the Bassmans or the use of 6L6s instead of 6V6s in the post-1957 Supers. This price analysis assumes the amp being considered has the most desirable circuit, which will always be the latter version.

The small amp trend affects even the prized narrow-panel tweeds. As you can see in Table 8 and Figure 7, the Bandmaster and Bassman—though worth more than all the other narrow-panel tweeds besides the HP and LP Twins—just aren't garnering much enthusiasm anymore. But the Princeton and Deluxe sure are!

The biggest surprise might be that the narrow-panel Pro was such a great investment 20 years ago. That's because it was much cheaper than the Deluxe in 2001. These days it's as desirable as the Deluxe but much harder to find.

Table 8. Narrow-Panel Amp Change in Value

Amp	10-y	20-y
Narrow-Panel Bandmaster (3x10)	-5%	**217%**
Narrow-Panel Bassman (4x10)	-10%	**157%**
Narrow-Panel Champ (1x8)	33%	**196%**
Narrow-Panel Deluxe (1x12)	43%	**200%**
Narrow-Panel Harvard (1x10)	5%	**156%**
Narrow-Panel Princeton (1x8)	50%	**182%**
Narrow-Panel Pro (1x15)	9%	**345%**
Narrow-Panel Super (2x10)	4%	**255%**
Narrow-Panel Tremolux (1x12)	-5%	**193%**
Narrow-Panel LP Twin (2x12)	17%	**286%**
Narrow-Panel HP Twin (2x12)	12%	**443%**
Narrow-Panel Vibrolux (1x10)	38%	**264%**

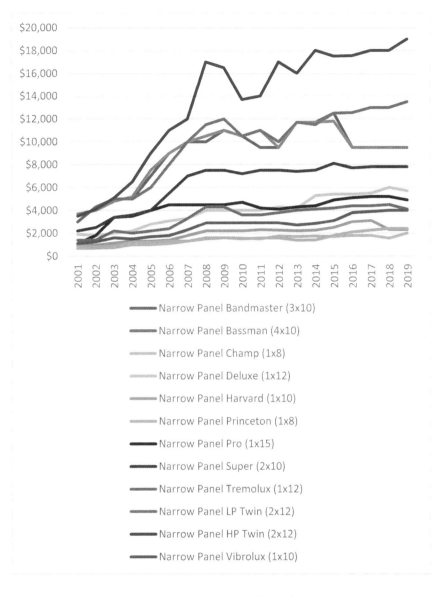

Figure 7. Narrow-Panel Tweeds

The Brown Amps (1961-1963)

The value of brown amps has risen nicely over the last 20 years (see Figure 8 and Table 9). Only one, however, has doubled in value since 2009. And that one would be the Princeton (of course). The two rarest ones—the 1963 Vibroverb and 3x10 Bandmaster—aren't as popular as they used to be. The brown Vibroverb is down 23% from its 2009 peak and the brown Bandmaster is down 42%. These were the only two vintage Fender amps that were hurt by over speculation. That's because their scarcity was so appealing. I guess they're not as rare anymore. I know of at least 4 brown Vibroverbs for sale as we speak. I also see brown Bandmasters come up for sale often. All I know is they're great amps and I'm happy to have both in my collection.

Figure 8 shows the most common versions of the brown amps. By that I mean it doesn't show the immensely rare early versions of some. For example, while the 1961 brown Bandmaster is worth $4,500, the 1960 "pink" center volume version is worth $8,000 (77% more). Try finding one of those. Oh, and while you're at it, see if the old lady also has the center volume Super in her cellar, too.

Jump into a time machine and buy yourself a plethora of brown Princetons. You'll get a better return for your money than if you filled the machine with narrow-panel Deluxes.

Table 9. Brown Amp Change in Value

Amp	10-y	20-y
Brown Bandmaster (3x10)	-42%	**50%**
Brown Concert (4x10)	0%	**88%**
Brown Deluxe (1x12)	19%	**237%**
Brown Princeton (1x10)	**100%**	**300%**
Brown Pro (1x15)	7%	**237%**
Brown Super (2x10)	24%	**77%**
Brown Vibrosonic (1x15)	3%	**121%**
Brown Vibrolux (1x12)	13%	**218%**
Brown Vibroverb (2x10)	-23%	**131%**

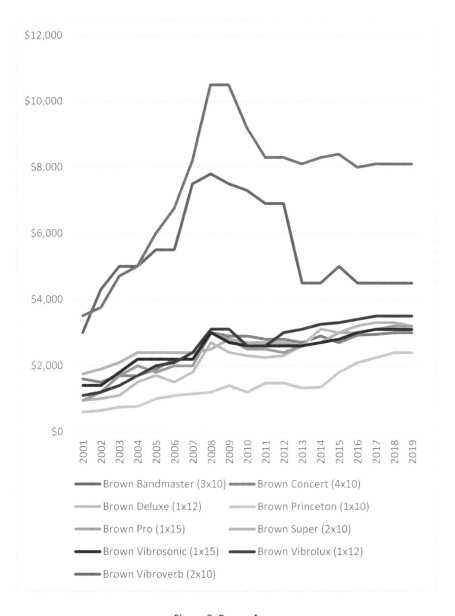

Figure 8. Brown Amps

The Black-Face Amps (1964-1967)

Yes, I know. Fender made black-face non-reverb versions of your favorite amps. In Figure 9 I just show the reverb models. The non-reverb amps will be included in individual model summaries later. Yes, they're theoretically rarer than their reverbed counterpart, but who wants a black-face Deluxe Amp when you can get a black-face Deluxe Reverb Amp for about the same price? Probably the rarest amp Fender ever made was the black-face Vibrolux (only in production for 3 months). But if you're a Vibrolux fan, you'll probably opt for the iconic Sultan of Swing brown version, which costs about the same.

All black-face models are shown in Table 10. Turns out the non-reverb models were great investments long ago. That's because they were inexpensive compared to their reverbed counterparts.

The 1964 "Tuxedo" version of the Princeton 6G2 is equivalent to the brown Princeton as far as this price analysis goes. I didn't distinguish between the two. The black-face Princeton shown in Table 10 and Figure 9 is the AA964 Princeton Amp.

There are many die-hard pre-CBS purists out there who insist that their faceplate say "Fender Elec. Instr. Co." and not "Fender Musical Instruments." The FEIC examples generally fetch a bit more than the FMI ones. Figure 8 doesn't factor in whether the black-face amp was made before or after 1965.

As you can see in Figure 9, the 1964 Vibroverb is the most expensive black-face amp you can add to your collection.

The low-power model trend continues. Deluxe Reverbs and Princeton Reverbs steadily climb in value while the other models just hover near their 2010 highs.

Table 10. Black-Face Amp Change in Value

Amp	10-y	20-y
Black-Face Bandmaster (Piggy Back)	-13%	56%
Black-Face Bassman (Piggy Back)	-3%	**106%**
Black-Face Champ (1x8)	13%	**100%**
Black-Face Concert (4x10)	14%	**159%**
Black-Face Deluxe (1x12)	24%	**343%**
Black-Face Deluxe Reverb (1x12)	23%	**129%**
Black-Face Dual Showman (Piggy Back)	8%	**170%**
Black-Face Princeton (1x10)	**124%**	280%
Black-Face Princeton Reverb (1x10)	88%	**276%**
Black-Face Pro (1x15)	-3%	**205%**
Black-Face Pro Reverb (2x12)	-9%	62%
Black-Face Showman 12 (Piggy Back)	-4%	**130%**
Black-Face Showman 15 (Piggy Back)	-4%	**130%**
Black-Face Super Reverb (4x10)	14%	56%
Black-Face Tremolux (Piggy Back)	51%	**225%**
Black-Face Twin Reverb (2x12)	0%	44%
Black-Face Vibro Champ (1x8)	36%	**138%**
Black-Face Vibrolux (1x12)	0%	**130%**
Black-Face Vibrolux Reverb (2x10)	14%	**100%**
Black-Face Vibroverb (1x15)	4%	**183%**

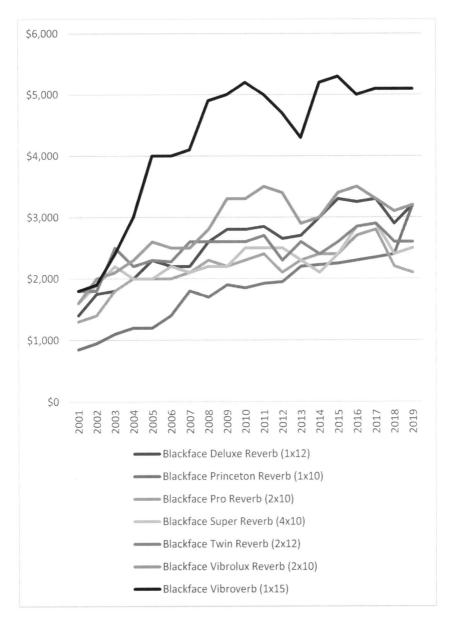

Figure 9. Black-Face Reverb Amps

The Silver-Face Amps (1968-1969)

I admit it. Years ago, I'd never get caught standing in front of a silver-face amp. I guess the only thing worse would have been to get caught standing in front of a silver-face amp with a 3-bolt neck Fender Stratocaster. These days, silver-face Fenders are recognized by the vintage amp consortium as being worthy of consideration. Everyone knows little changed on the Fullerton assembly line between 1967 and 1969. Since these amps sell for quite a bit less than their one year older black-face siblings (see Figure 10), someone not influenced by CBS's cost cutting bad reputation might actually find a great amp for a great price.

The data for Figure 10 and Table 11 includes only amps made during the first silver-face era (these are the so-called "drip edge" models). Fender amps made after 1969 were notorious for poor craftsmanship. The cost saving designs pushed through by the corporate bigwigs steering the Fender sinking ship affected the amps most of all.

Again, as with the other eras, smaller is better. Maybe one day I'll soften my hard-hearted ways and try a silver-face Deluxe or Princeton Reverb. I used to swear I'd never play a post-CBS Strat or Tele. But now I do. Maybe a silver-face amp is also in the cards.

Table 11. Silver-Face Amp Change in Value

Amp	10-y	20-y
Silver-Face Bandmaster (Piggy Back)	-8%	54%
Silver-Face Bassman (Piggy Back)	-8%	85%
Silver-Face Champ (1x8)	47%	**144%**
Silver-Face Deluxe Reverb (1x12)	28%	**283%**
Silver-Face Dual Showman (Piggy Back)	-13%	40%
Silver-Face Princeton Reverb (1x10)	25%	**150%**
Silver-Face Pro Reverb (2x12)	39%	**200%**
Silver-Face Showman 15 (Piggy Back)	-9%	43%
Silver-Face Super Reverb (4x10)	0%	**100%**
Silver-Face Twin Reverb (2x12)	14%	39%
Silver-Face Vibro Champ (1x8)	39%	**150%**
Silver-Face Vibrolux Reverb (2x10)	50%	**167%**

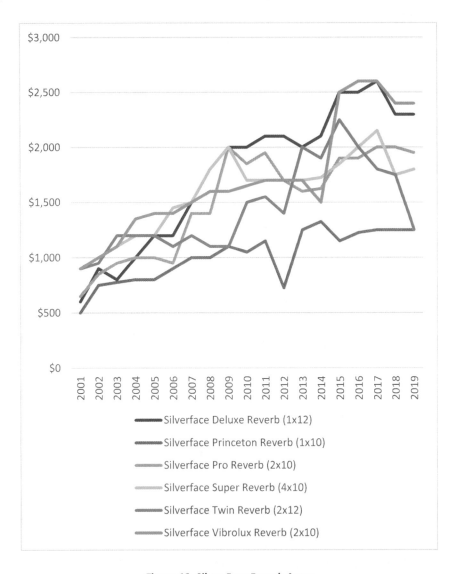

Figure 10. Silver-Face Reverb Amps

The Bandmaster

Let's now look at the individual models.

The Bandmaster is an iconic amp. It started out as one of three 1x15 "big cowboy" amps and then mysteriously switched to the 3x10 version everyone loves. That version—sadly—lasted only a few years and then the Bandmaster became the somewhat forgotten about piggy back. Oh, the humanity.

As you can see in Figure 11, the narrow-panel 3x10 is the one to have. Dare I say it? I might as well. This version of the Bandmaster is my favorite Fender amp of all time. As of today, it's off its peak value, down 24% from its 2015 high. Suspiciously, the narrow-panel Bassman is also down 24% from its 2015 high. Are people really shunning even the bigger "best ever" Fender amps these days? I guess so.

Wide-panel and brown versions of the Bandmaster were cherished by generations of guitar players. Now, they just seem to hold their value, keeping their heads slightly above the boutique amp line ($4,000). The brown version had a surge in 2007 and then returned to $4,000. It's down 35% from its 2012 high.

The Bandmaster piggy backs sell for roughly half of what the Bassmans and Showmans do. Is there a lesson in there somewhere? Probably.

Table 12. Bandmaster Amp Change in Value

Amp	10-y	20-y
Wide-Panel Bandmaster (1x15)	-12%	38%
Narrow Panel Bandmaster (3x10)	-5%	**217%**
Brown Bandmaster (3x10)	-42%	50%
Blonde Bandmaster (Piggy Back)	8%	86%
Black-Face Bandmaster (Piggy Back)	-13%	56%
Silver-Face Bandmaster (Piggy Back)	-8%	54%

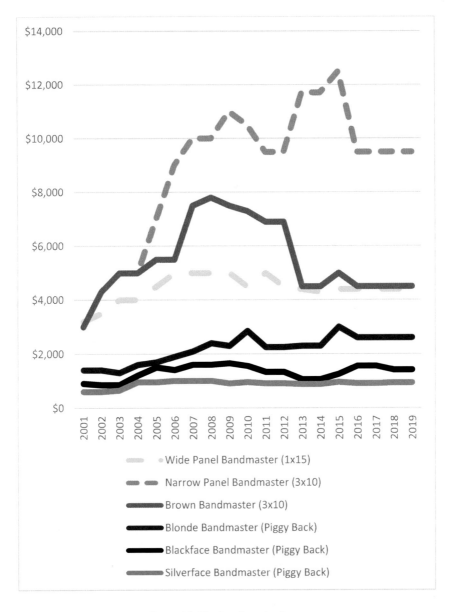

Figure 11. The Bandmaster Amps

The Bassman

Gee, Figure 12 looks an awful lot like Figure 11. These days the narrow-panel Bandmasters and Bassmans track identically. How ironic is it that the two greatest amps of all time had such short production lives. Leo Fender, ever the forward thinker, wasn't thinking about Bassmans and Bandmasters when the Tolex and JBL salesmen's cards were snapped into his desk rolodex roll. He moved on and so did the rest of us I guess.

More has been written about the 5E6-A Bassman than just about any other amp in history. Is it the greatest guitar amp of all time? Sure. Well, that is until you play a 5E7 Bandmaster. Since both cost about the same, why not go with the Bandmaster? It's a much rarer and better sounding amp.

Blondes do have more fun. The blonde piggy back is now a better investment than the iconic narrow-panel tweed version.

Table 13. Bassman Amp Change in Value

Amp	10-y	20-y
TV-Front Bassman (1x15)	-40%	15%
Wide-Panel Bassman (1x15)	-38%	35%
Narrow-Panel Bassman (4x10)	-10%	**157%**
Blonde Bassman (Piggy Back)	39%	**200%**
Black-Face Bassman (Piggy Back)	-3%	**106%**
Silver-Face Bassman (Piggy Back)	-8%	85%

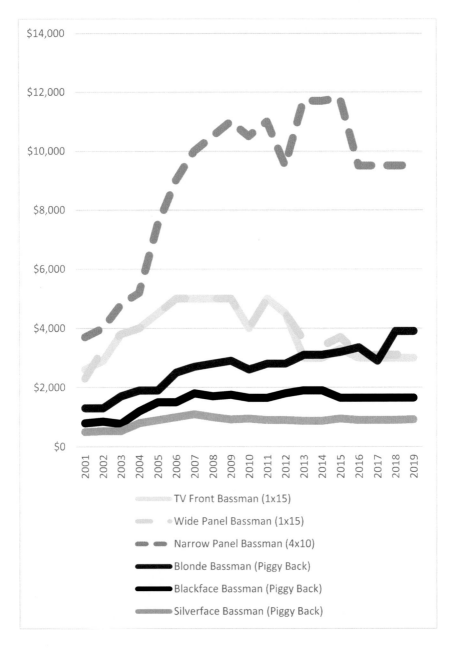

Figure 12. The Bassman Amps

The Champ

If I learned anything while making *Naked and Dimed*, it was that the Champ is a champ. Nothing—*nothing*—will make you sound more like a guitar God than this little 4-watt single-ended compression machine. Figure 13 shows that the small tweed amp trend is even obeyed by something well-born guitarists call a student model. I suggest you get one now if you don't have one.

Table 14. Champ Amp Change in Value

Amp	10-y	20-y
Wide-Panel Champ (1x6)	32%	**154%**
Narrow-Panel Champ (1x8)	33%	**196%**
Black-Face Champ (1x8)	13%	**100%**
Silver-Face Champ (1x8)	47%	**144%**
Black-Face Vibro Champ (1x8)	36%	**138%**
Silver-Face Vibro Champ (1x8)	39%	**150%**

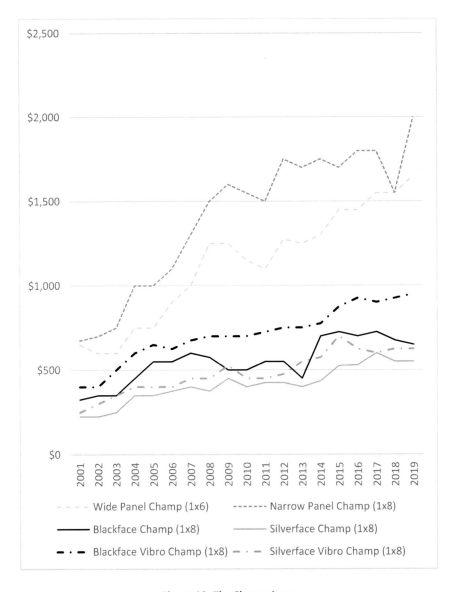

Figure 13. The Champ Amps

The Deluxe

The Deluxe will always be one of my favorite Fender amps. Why? Because it has all the little things that add up to make me sound my best when I'm playing the style of music I play. The Deluxe sometimes seems to be more of a musical instrument than my guitar. It really is the greatest little signal processor ever designed for that bland little sine wave coming out of your black-bottomed pickups.

The narrow-panel Deluxe is the most valuable of the Deluxes (big surprise there). It's safe to say it will only get more expensive as the small amp trend continues.

Actually, remember when I told you to fill your time machine with brown Princetons? Maybe throw a few black-face Deluxe Amps and silver-face Deluxe Reverbs in there, too.

Table 15. Deluxe Amp Change in Value

Amp	10-y	20-y
TV-Front Deluxe (1x12)	52%	**133%**
Wide-Panel Deluxe (1x12)	17%	**119%**
Narrow-Panel Deluxe (1x12)	43%	**200%**
Brown Deluxe (1x12)	19%	**237%**
Black-Face Deluxe (1x12)	24%	**343%**
Black-Face Deluxe Reverb (1x12)	23%	**129%**
Silver-Face Deluxe Reverb (1x12)	28%	**283%**

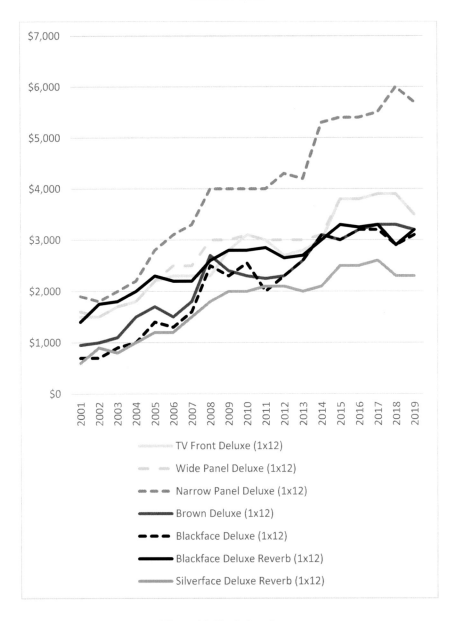

Figure 14. The Deluxe Amps

The Princeton

The Princeton amps are shown in Figure 15 and Table 16. As you can see, they're now a hot commodity. The brown Princeton, black-face Princeton Amp, and Princeton Reverb appear to be the ones everyone wants. If you don't have at least a brown Princeton, I don't know what to tell you. Get one now before they climb over $2,500.

I don't know if the recent spike in the value of the Princeton Reverb is a blip or not, but chances are people are now wise to the fact that these are awesome amps. They cost as much as Deluxe Reverbs and Vibrolux Reverbs now.

Table 16. Princeton Amp Change in Value

Amp	10-y	20-y
TV-Front Princeton (1x8)	58%	81%
Wide-Panel Princeton (1x8)	58%	**100%**
Narrow-Panel Princeton (1x8)	50%	**182%**
Brown Princeton (1x10)	**100%**	**300%**
Black-Face Princeton (1x10)	**124%**	**280%**
Black-Face Princeton Reverb (1x10)	88%	**276%**
Silver-Face Princeton Reverb (1x10)	25%	**150%**

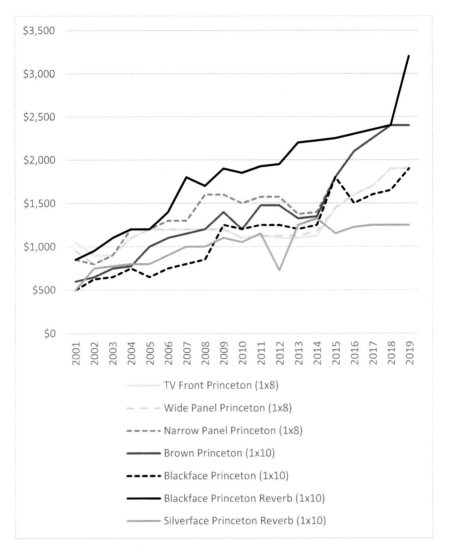

Figure 15. The Princeton Amps

The Pro

The Pro amps have always had a special place in the hearts of guitar players who want to be heard over the din of fiddles and mandolins. As shown in Figure 16, the tweeds will always be in demand. You might also notice that the Pro Reverb is down near the $2,000 line. If you don't have one, now would be the time to bring one home to meet the family.

Table 17. Pro Amp Change in Value

Amp	10-y	20-y
TV-Front Pro (1x15)	-5%	**147%**
Wide-Panel Pro (1x15)	0%	**186%**
Narrow-Panel Pro (1x15)	9%	**345%**
Brown Pro (1x15)	7%	**237%**
Black-Face Pro (1x15)	-3%	**205%**
Black-Face Pro Reverb (2x12)	-9%	62%
Silver-Face Pro Reverb (2x12)	39%	**200%**

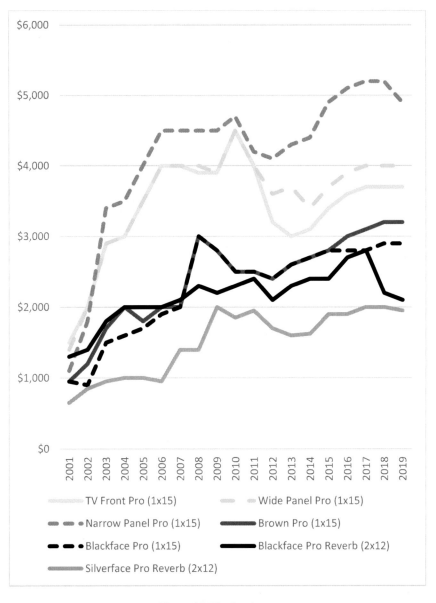

Figure 16. The Pro Amps

The Showman

If you must, you must. The Rendezvous Ballroom doesn't exist anymore but if you're looking to impress the VFW Hall gang, why not do it with a Showman? The blonde Tolex ones will always be the ones that guitar slingers want most. The graph below (Figure 17) shows the oxblood grill version for the blondes. The straw-colored grills go for a bit less.

Table 18. Showman Amp Change in Value

Amp	10-y	20-y
Blonde Dual Showman (Piggy Back)	-2%	**227%**
Black-Face Dual Showman (Piggy Back)	8%	**170%**
Silver-Face Dual Showman (Piggy Back)	-13%	40%
Blonde Showman 12 (Piggy Back)	0%	**200%**
Black-Face Showman 12 (Piggy Back)	-4%	**130%**
Blonde Showman 15 (Piggy Back)	-7%	91%
Black-Face Showman 15 (Piggy Back)	-4%	**130%**
Silver-Face Showman 15 (Piggy Back)	-9%	43%

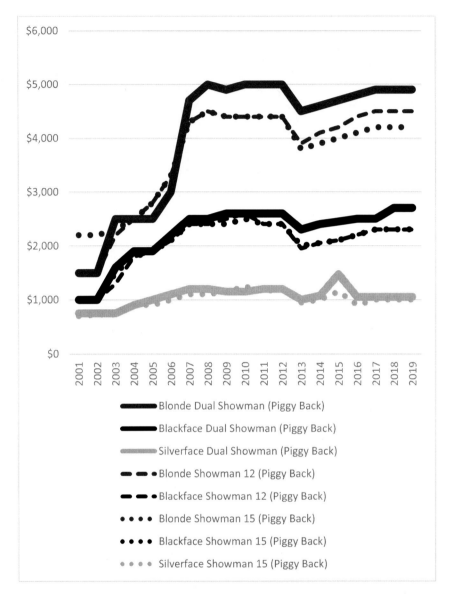

Figure 17. The Showman Amps

The Super

Like I said before, the narrow-panel 18-35 watt 6L6 wonders are my favorite amps of all time. The Super and Pro are the most affordable (but are hard to find). The late '50s Super has hovered steadily around $8,000 for the last ten years (See Figure 18). Compare that to the late '50s Pro (hovering under $5,000). The others are all above $9,000.

Super Reverbs hold their value. Sadly, they're now the poster child for the "too loud and heavy" category. If you have a hankering for a loud black-face amp that costs less than $2,000 you might be better served to buy a Pro Reverb.

Table 19. Super Amp Change in Value

Amp	10-y	20-y
V-Front Super (2x10)	38%	**110%**
Wide-Panel Super (2x10)	2%	**132%**
Narrow-Panel Super (2x10)	4%	**255%**
Brown Super (2x10)	24%	77%
Black-Face Super Reverb (4x10)	14%	56%
Silver-Face Super Reverb (4x10)	0%	**100%**

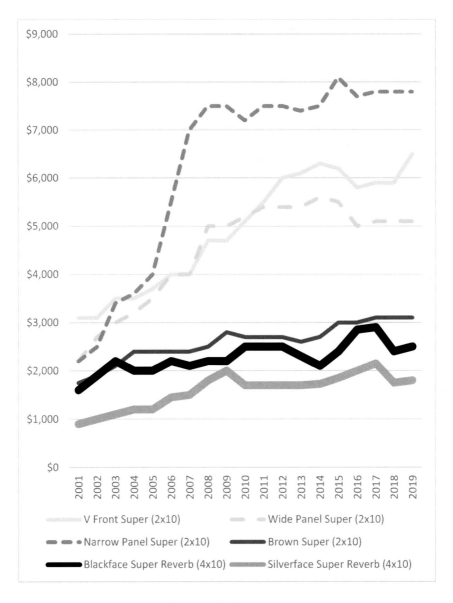

Figure 18. The Super Amps

The Tremolux

Figure 19 shows the Tremolux amps. Like many of the narrow-panel tweeds, they shot up in value in 2006. They've kind of hovered about the $4,000 mark for the last ten years.

The Tremolux piggy backs have always been popular. They were kind of marketed as the entry level piggy back for those wanting to look like Dick Dale on a surf bum's weekly allowance.

Table 20. Tremolux Amp Change in Value

Amp	10-y	20-y
Narrow-Panel Tremolux (1x12)	-5%	**193%**
Blonde Tremolux (Piggy Back)	0%	**189%**
Black-Face Tremolux (Piggy Back)	51%	**225%**

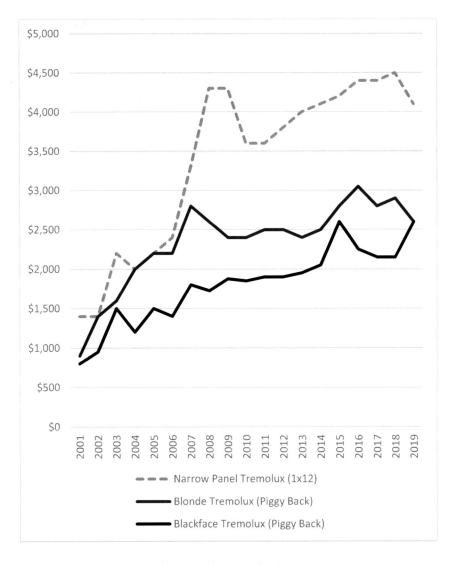

Figure 19. The Tremolux Amps

The Twin

Remember all that I said about your time machine earlier? Forget it. Set the dial for 1959. No doubt you'll be wedging Les Pauls and Stratocasters between Fender Twin amps before you return. Maybe you'll be wise and toss in Picasso's *El Bobo* too. If you look at Figure 20 you'll see all Twins models appreciated considerably except for the Twin Reverbs. Oddly, what you paid for a Twin Reverb in 2001 is about what you'd pay for one now. The Twin Reverb joins the Fender Reverb Unit and any 1930's National steel guitar for musical instruments that will never go up or down in price. You could add it to the Office of Weights and Measures as a monetary benchmark.

Table 21. Twin Amp Change in Value

Amp	10-y	20-y
Wide-Panel Twin (2x12)	34%	**168%**
Narrow-Panel LP Twin (2x12)	17%	**286%**
Narrow-Panel HP Twin (2x12)	12%	**443%**
Blonde Twin (2x12)	0%	**183%**
Black-Face Twin Reverb (2x12)	0%	44%
Silver-Face Twin Reverb (2x12)	14%	39%

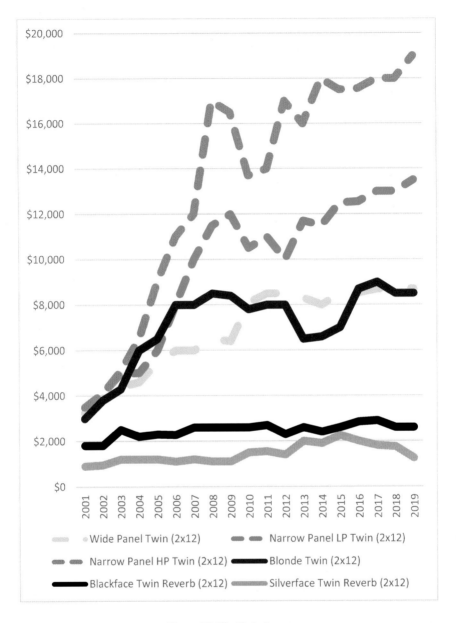

Figure 20. The Twin Amps

The Vibrolux

Figure 21 shows the values of the Vibrolux amps. They've gone up steadily over the last 20 years. The narrow-panel tweed did what the Tremolux narrow-panel tweed did, increasing around 4 times in value. That was a better investment than the Low Power Twin.

Table 22. Vibrolux Amp Change in Value

Amp	10-y	20-y
Narrow Panel Vibrolux (1x10)	38%	**264%**
Brown Vibrolux (1x12)	13%	**218%**
Black-Face Vibrolux (1x12)	0%	**130%**
Black-Face Vibrolux Reverb (2x10)	14%	**100%**
Silver-Face Vibrolux Reverb (2x10)	50%	**167%**

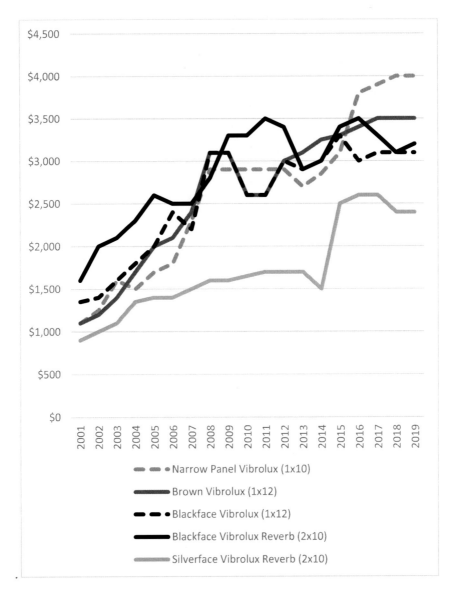

Figure 21. The Vibrolux Amps

The Professional Series Browns

Fender started marketing amps for "professionals" when the brown amps debuted. The first one was the 40 watt Vibrasonic. Then came the 40 watt Concert. The brown Pro, Vibrolux and Vibroverbs all had very similar circuits. The only difference was the OT and speaker configuration. Figure 22 shows the "Professional Series" amps. They basically all track the same.

Table 23. Brown Professional Series Amp Change in Value

Amp	10-y	20-y
Brown Concert (4x10)	0%	88%
Brown Pro (1x15)	7%	**237%**
Brown Super (2x10)	24%	77%
Brown Vibrosonic (1x15)	3%	**121%**

Figure 22. The Professional Series Browns

The 2x10 Fender Amps

If you're curious how the 2x10 amps compare, have a look at Figure 23. Is the brown Vibroverb and narrow-panel Super really about the same price these days? I guess so. The Vibroverb will get more likes on Facebook but true ampoholics know that late '50s Supers will make the hair stand up on the back of their neck. Your call.

If you have a Vibrolux Reverb, do you even need a Vibroverb? I hate to say this but probably not.

Table 24. 2x10 Amp Change in Value

Amp	10-y	20-y
V-Front Dual Professional (2x10)	18%	94%
V-Front Super (2x10)	38%	**110%**
Wide-Panel Super (2x10)	2%	**132%**
Narrow-Panel Super (2x10)	4%	**255%**
Brown Super (2x10)	24%	77%
Black-Face Vibrolux Reverb (2x10)	14%	**100%**
Silver-Face Vibrolux Reverb (2x10)	50%	**167%**
Brown Vibroverb (2x10)	-23%	**131%**

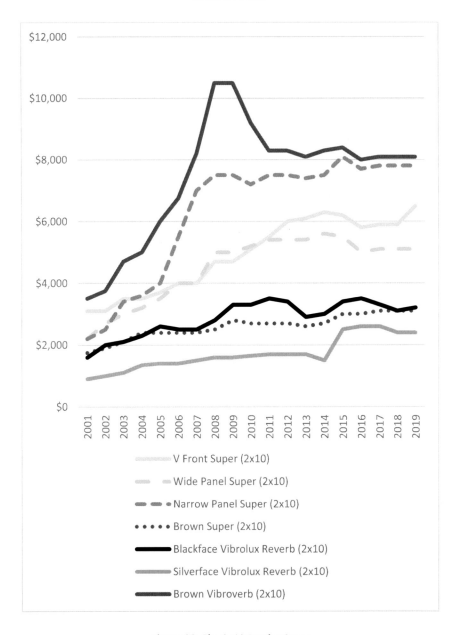

Figure 23. The 2x10 Fender Amps

The 4x10 Fender Amps

Since I wasted your time showing you 2x10 amps, I might as well waste it showing you the 4x10s (see Figure 24). Any surprises there? No.

Table 25. 4x10 Amp Change in Value

Amp	10-y	20-y
Narrow Panel Bassman (4x10)	-10%	**157%**
Brown Concert (4x10)	0%	88%
Black-Face Concert (4x10)	14%	**159%**
Black-Face Super Reverb (4x10)	14%	56%
Silver-Face Super Reverb (4x10)	0%	**100%**

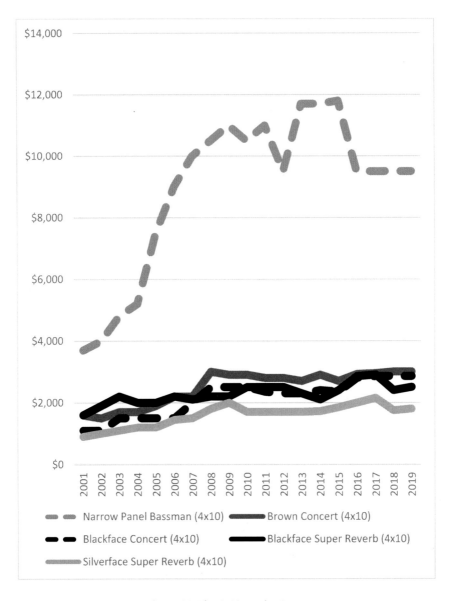

Figure 24. The 4x10 Fender Amps

Photo Credits

Joel Klein: Cover, Pages iii, 13, 19, 23, 26, 27, 31, 37, 48, 53, 55, 59, 61, 65, 67, 69, 70, 71, 73, 75, 77, 82, 85, 86, 91, 93, 99, 101, 105, 113, 116 (top), 123, 125, 126, 129, 131, 132, 135, 141, 151, 157, 159, 163, 169, 172, 175, 177 (top), and 182
George Binkley: Page 29
Reed Munns: Pages 34, 35, and 39
Mark Lovett: Page 49 and 50
Shane Matsumoto: Page 72
Tommie James: Pages 110, 111, 116 (bottom), 117, 137 (top), 138, 143, 171, 177 (bottom), 178, 184, and 185

All other photos taken by the author.

References

Tony Bacon, *The Stratocaster Guitar Book: A Complete History of Fender Stratocaster Guitars,* Backbeat; Reprint edition (October 1, 2010).

Nacho Baños, *The Blackguard,* N. Baños (2005).

J. W. Black, *The Fender Bass: An Illustrated History,* Hal Leonard (Oct 1, 2001).

Bill Blackburn, *Old Guitar Mania,* Centerstream Publications (March 1, 1992).

Deke Dickerson, *The Strat in the Attic,* Voyageur Press; First edition (June 1, 2013).

Andre R. Duchoissoir, *The Fender Stratocaster 1954-1984,* Hal Leonard (1985).

Andre R. Duchoissoir, *Fender Telecaster; The Detailed Story of America's Senior Solid Body Electric Guitar,* Hal Leonard; 1st edition (1991).

Ritchie Fliegler, *Amps!: The Other Half of Rock 'N' Roll,* Hal Leonard; First edition (November 1, 1993).

Allen Greenwood, *The Official Vintage Guitar Magazine Price Guide 2019,* Vintage Guitar Music (Oct, 2018).

Allen Greenwood, *The Official Vintage Guitar Magazine Price Guide 2018,* Vintage Guitar Music (Oct, 2017).

Allen Greenwood, *The Official Vintage Guitar Magazine Price Guide 2017,* Vintage Guitar Music (Oct, 2016).

Allen Greenwood, *The Official Vintage Guitar Magazine Price Guide 2016,* Vintage Guitar Music (Oct, 2015).

Allen Greenwood, *The Official Vintage Guitar Magazine Price Guide 2015,* Vintage Guitar Music (Oct, 2014).

Allen Greenwood, *The Official Vintage Guitar Magazine Price Guide 2014,* Vintage Guitar Music (Oct, 2013).

Allen Greenwood, *The Official Vintage Guitar Magazine Price Guide 2013,* Vintage Guitar Music (Oct, 2012).

Allen Greenwood, *The Official Vintage Guitar Magazine Price Guide 2012,* Vintage Guitar Music (Oct, 2011).

Allen Greenwood, *The Official Vintage Guitar Magazine Price Guide 2011,* Vintage Guitar Music (Oct, 2010).

Allen Greenwood, *The Official Vintage Guitar Magazine Price Guide 2010,* Vintage Guitar Music (Oct, 2009).

Allen Greenwood, *The Official Vintage Guitar Magazine Price Guide 2009,* Vintage Guitar Music (Oct, 2008).

Allen Greenwood, *The Official Vintage Guitar Magazine Price Guide 2008,* Vintage Guitar Music (Oct, 2007).

Allen Greenwood, *The Official Vintage Guitar Magazine Price Guide 2007,* Vintage Guitar Music (Oct, 2006).

Allen Greenwood, *The Official Vintage Guitar Magazine Price Guide 2006,* Vintage Guitar Music (Oct, 2005).

Allen Greenwood, *The Official Vintage Guitar Magazine Price Guide 2005,* Vintage Guitar Music (Oct, 2004).

Allen Greenwood, *The Official Vintage Guitar Magazine Price Guide 2004,* Vintage Guitar Music (Oct, 2003).

Allen Greenwood, *The Official Vintage Guitar Magazine Price Guide 2003,* Vintage Guitar Music (Oct, 2002).

Allen Greenwood, *The Official Vintage Guitar Magazine Price Guide 2002,* Vintage Guitar Music (Oct, 2001).

Allen Greenwood, *The Official Vintage Guitar Magazine Price Guide 2001,* Vintage Guitar Music (Oct, 2000).

George Gruhn, *Gruhn's Guide to Vintage Guitars,* Backbeat; Third edition (March 1, 2010).

Dave Hunter, *365 Guitars, Amps & Affects You Must Play: The Most Sublime, Bizarre and Outrageous Gear Ever*, Voyageur Press; First edition (May 15, 2013).

Dave Hunter, *Amped: The Illustrated History of the World's Greatest Amplifiers*, Voyageur Press; First edition (May 7, 2012).

Dave Hunter, *The Guitar Amp Handbook: Understanding Tube Amplifiers and Getting Great Sounds*, Backbeat; Updated edition (May 1, 2015).

Dave Hunter, *The Fender Stratocaster: The Life and Times of the World's Greatest Guitar and it's Players,* Voyageur Press; First edition (November 16, 2013).

Dave Hunter, *The Fender Telecaster: The Life and Times of the Electric Guitar That Changed the World,* Voyageur Press; Reprint edition (August 1, 2015).

Dave Hunter, *The Gibson Les Paul: The Illustrated History of the Guitar that Changed Rock,* Voyageur Press (June 15, 2014).

Dave Hunter, *Tone Manual: Discovering Your Ultimate Electric Guitar Sound,* Hal Leonard Corporation; Pap/Com edition (April 1, 2011).

Martin Kelly, Paul Kelly, and Terry Foster, *Fender: The Golden Age 1946-1970*, Cassell Illustrated (2011).

Robert Megantz, *Design and Construction of Tube Guitar Amplifiers*, TacTec Press; 3rd edition (September 1, 2009).

John Morrish, *The Fender Amp Book*, Backbeat Books; 1st Amer. edition (February 1, 1995).

Aspen Pittman, *The Tube Amp Book*, Backbeat; Deluxe Revised edition (September 1, 2003).

RCA Air Cooled Transmitting Tubes, Technical Manual TT3 (1938).

RCA Receiving Tube Manual - Technical Series RC 24 (1965).

Detlef Schmidt, *Fender Precision Basses: 1951-1954,* Centerstream Publications (June 1, 2010).

Richard Smith, *Fender: The Sound Heard 'Round the World,* Hal Leonard; Har/DVD Ce edition (February 1, 2010)

John Teagle and John Sprung, *Fender Amps: The First Fifty Years*, Hal Leonard Corp (July 1, 1995)

Doug Tulloch, *Neptune Bound: The Ultimate Danelectro Guitar Guide,* Centerstream Publications; 1st edition (December 1, 2008).

Tom Wheeler, *The Soul of Tone: Celebrating 60 Years of Fender Amps*, Hal Leonard; First Edition (October 15, 2007).

Tom Wheeler, *The Stratocaster Chronicles: Celebrating 50 Years of the Fender Strat,* Hal Leonard; Har/Com edition (April 1, 2004).

Tom Wheeler, *The Guitar Book: A Handbook for Electric and Acoustic Guitarists*, Harper & Row; 1st edition (1974).

DID YOU ENJOY THIS BOOK?

Please consider giving it a review on Amazon.com

Be sure to read all of Ram Tuli's books. They're available on Amazon in both Kindle and paperback formats.

The Harding Hall Mysteries

Dying Horribly at Harding Hall (2016)
Footsteps in the Fog (2017)
The Mango Tree (2018)
As Luck Would Have It (2018)

The Steaming Books

King Paul's Big, Nasty Unofficial Book of Reactor and Engineering Memories, Vol. 1 (2018)
King Paul's Big, Nasty Unofficial Book of Reactor and Engineering Memories, Vol. 2 (2018)
King Paul's Big, Nasty Unofficial Book of Reactor and Engineering Memories, Vol. 3 (2018)
King Paul's Big, Nasty Unofficial Book of Reactor and Engineering Memories, Vol. 4 (2019)
King Paul's Big, Nasty Unofficial Book of Reactor and Engineering Memories, Vol. 5 (2019)
King Paul's Big, Nasty Unofficial Book of Reactor and Engineering Memories, Vol. 6 (2019)
King Paul's Big, Nasty Unofficial Book of Reactor and Engineering Memories, Vol. 7 (2019)

Mooj Books

The Complete Enlightenment Part 1 (2019)
The Complete Enlightenment Part 2 (2019)
The Complete Enlightenment Part 3 (2019)

Guitar and Amp Books

Naked and Dimed, My Life-Long Quest for Awesome Tone (2019)

Made in the USA
Las Vegas, NV
22 November 2020

11302730R00157